Ray Monk is Professor of Philosophy at the University of Southampton. He is the author of *Ludwig Wittgenstein: The Duty of Genius* and a two-volume biography of Bertrand Russell.

HOW TO READ

HOW
TO
READ

WITTGENSTEIN

RAY MONK

W. W. Norton & Company
New York   London

First published in Great Britain by Granta Publications

Tractatus Logico-Philosophicus by Ludwig Wittgenstein, translated by Pears and
McGuinness, 1975, Routledge. *Logic and Knowledge* by Bertrand Russell, 1957,
Routledge, The Bertrand Russell Peace Foundation. *Blue and Brown Books:
Preliminary Studies for the 'Philosophical Investigations'* by Ludwig Wittgenstein,
translated by G. E. M. Anscombe, Blackwell Publishing. *Philosophical Investigations* by
Ludwig Wittgenstein, translated by G. E. M. Anscombe, Blackwell Publishing.
Philosophical Remarks by Ludwig Wittgenstein, edited by Rush Rhees, translated by
R. Hargreaves and R. White, Blackwell Publishing. *Last Writings on the Philosophy of
Psychology* by Wittgenstein, ed. Von Wright and Heikki Nyman, translated by
Luckhard, Vols I and II, Blackwell Publishing. *Letters to Russell, Keynes, and More*, ed.
Von Wright, Blackwell Publishing. Used with kind permission.

For information about permission to reproduce selections from
this book, write to Permissions, W. W. Norton & Company, Inc.,
500 Fifth Avenue, New York, N.Y. 10110

Manufacturing by The Maple-Vail Book Manufacturing Group
Production manager: Amanda Morrison

Library of Congress Cataloging-in-Publication Data

Monk, Ray.
How to read Wittgenstein / Ray Monk.—1st American ed.
p. cm.—(How to read)
Includes bibliographical references and index.
ISBN 0-393-32820-1 (pbk.)
1. Wittgenstein, Ludwig, 1889–1951. I. Title.
II. Series: How to read (New York, N.Y.)
B3376.W564M66 2005
192—dc22
2005019289

W. W. Norton & Company, Inc.
500 Fifth Avenue, New York, N.Y. 10110
www.wwnorton.com

W. W. Norton & Company Ltd.
Castle House, 75/76 Wells Street, London W1T 3QT

CONTENTS

SERIES EDITOR'S FOREWORD

How am I to read *How to Read*?

This series is based on a very simple, but novel idea. Most beginners' guides to great thinkers and writers offer either potted biography or condensed summaries of their major works, or perhaps even both. *How to Read*, by contrast, brings the reader face-to-face with the writing itself in the company of an expert guide. Its starting point is that in order to get close to what a writer is all about, you have to get close to the words they actually use and be shown how to read those words.

Every book in the series is in a way a masterclass in reading. Each author has selected ten or so short extracts from a writer's work and looks at them in detail as a way of revealing their central ideas and thereby opening doors on to a whole world of thought. Sometimes these extracts are arranged chronologically to give a sense of a thinker's development over time, sometimes not. The books are not merely compilations of a thinker's most famous passages, their 'greatest hits', but rather they offer a series of clues or keys that will enable readers to go on and make discoveries of their own. In addition to the texts and readings, each book provides a short biographical chronology and suggestions for further reading and so on. The books in the *How to Read* series don't claim to tell you all you need to know about Freud, Nietzsche and Darwin, or indeed Shakespeare and the Marquis de Sade, but they do offer the best starting point for further exploration.

Unlike the available second-hand versions of the minds that have shaped our intellectual, cultural, religious, political and scientific landscape, *How to Read* offers a refreshing set of first-hand encounters with those minds. Our hope is that these books will, by turn, instruct, intrigue, embolden, encourage and delight.

Simon Critchley
New School for Social Research, New York

INTRODUCTION

Ludwig Wittgenstein (1889–1951) was by universal agreement one of greatest and one of the most influential philosophers of the twentieth century. There, however, the agreement stops. The question of *how to read* him is one that has excited a great deal of controversy ever since his first book, *Tractatus Logico-Philosophicus*, was published in 1921. There is no consensus on how that book should be interpreted, or on how his later work, *Philosophical Investigations*, ought to be read, or again on the extent to which the later work repudiates the earlier.

In this context, it is extremely presumptuous to publish a book called *How to Read Wittgenstein*. I apologize in advance for doing so and want to make it clear that what I offer here is only *one possible way* of reading Wittgenstein.

The extracts from Wittgenstein's own writings that are reproduced and discussed below are arranged in broadly chronological order and I give some biographical details in amongst the commentary that I offer. However, it might be as well to begin with a summary.

Wittgenstein was born in Vienna in 1889 into one of the wealthiest families of the Austro-Hungarian Empire. His father was an industrialist who owned practically the whole of the Austrian iron and steel industry. Under his father's influence, Wittgenstein studied engineering, first at Berlin and then at Manchester, but then became gripped by philosophical questions and came to Cambridge in the autumn of 1911 to study with Bertrand Russell. Wittgenstein quickly became Russell's favourite pupil and the one to whom Russell looked for a solution to the unresolved questions in the philosophy of logic. In 1913, Wittgenstein left Cambridge to live alone in Norway, hoping that the solitude would help his concentration. He spent a year there, thinking about logic, before returning to Vienna on the eve of the First World War.

During the war, Wittgenstein served in the Austrian army and, at the end of the war, was taken prisoner by the Italians. By that time, he had finished *Tractatus Logico-Philosophicus*, which, however, was not published until 1921. Thinking he had, in that book, solved all philosophical problems, Wittgenstein gave up philosophy and became a schoolteacher. His time as a teacher was short, unsuccessful and miserable and in 1926 he switched to being an architect, before, in 1929, returning to Cambridge to work on philosophy again, having become convinced that the *Tractatus* did not, after all, provide the final solution to all the problems of philosophy.

From 1929 until his death in 1951, Wittgenstein worked out a new way of doing philosophy that has no precedent in the history of the subject. It is a way of approaching philosophy that tries to remain faithful to the insight he had in the *Tractatus* that philosophy *cannot* be a science, or anything like a science. It is not a body of doctrine but an activity, the activity of clearing up the confusions caused by the bewitchments cast by language.

This conception of the subject is, in my opinion, Wittgenstein's most radical and most important contribution to philosophy.

LOGIC, SCIENCE AND BUSINESS

The Science of Logic: an inquiry into the principles of accurate thought and scientific method. By P. Coffey, Ph.D. (Louvain). Professor of Logic and Metaphysics, Maynooth College. Longmans, Green & Co. 1912.

In no branch of learning can an author disregard the results of honest research with so much impunity as he can in Philosophy and Logic. To this circumstance we owe the publication of such a book as Mr Coffey's 'Science of Logic': and only as a typical example of the work of many logicians today does this book deserve consideration. The author's Logic is that of the scholastic philosophers and he makes all their mistakes – of course with the usual references to Aristotle. (Aristotle, whose name is so much taken in vain by our logicians, would turn in his grave if he knew that so many Logicians know no more about Logic to-day than he did 2,000 years ago.) The author has not taken the slightest notice of the great work of the modern mathematical logicians – work which has brought about an advance in Logic comparable only to that which made Astronomy out of Astrology, and Chemistry out of Alchemy.

Mr Coffey, like many logicians, draws a great advantage from an unclear way of expressing himself; for if you cannot tell whether he means to say 'Yes' or 'No', it is difficult to argue against him. However, even through his foggy expression, many grave mistakes can be recognized clearly enough; and I propose to give a list of some of the most striking ones, and would advise the student of Logic to trace these mistakes and their consequences in other books on Logic also. (The numbers in brackets indicate the pages of Mr Coffey's book – Volume 1 – where a mistake occurs for the first time; the illustrative examples are my own.)

I.   [36] The author believes that all propositions are of the subject-predicate form.

II.   [31] He believes that reality is changed by becoming an object of thoughts.

III.   [6] He confounds the copula 'is' with the word 'is' expressing identity. (The word 'is' has obviously different meanings in the propositions –
'Twice two is four'
and 'Socrates is mortal.')

IV.   [46] He confounds things with the classes to which they belong. (A man is obviously something quite different from mankind.)

V.   [48] He confounds classes and complexes. (Mankind is a class whose elements are men; but a library is not a class whose elements are books, because books become parts of a library only by standing in certain spatial relations to one another – while classes are independent of the relations between their members.)

VI.   [47] He confounds complexes and sums. (Two plus two is four, but four is not a complex of two and itself.)

This list of mistakes could be extended a good deal.
The worst of such books as this is that they prejudice sen-
    sible people against the study of Logic.

Cambridge Review, 1913

Wittgenstein's published output was tiny. In his lifetime, he
published just one book, one article and one book review.
This (the above) is the book review. It was published in 1913
in a Cambridge undergraduate magazine called the *Cambridge
Review*, and was his very first publication. Wittgenstein was
then a student of philosophy at Trinity College, Cambridge,
halfway through his second year of study. In many ways,
though, it would be misleading to picture him at this time as
an undergraduate student, or, in any case, it would be misleading to think of him as, in any sense, an 'ordinary'
undergraduate student. For one thing, at twenty-four, he was
a few years older than the usual second-year undergraduate,
having spent three years before he went to Cambridge as an
engineering student in Manchester. For another thing, he
was already regarded by two of the most influential philosophers of the day, G.E. Moore and Bertrand Russell, as a
significant philosopher in his own right. Indeed, when
Wittgenstein's sister, Hermine, visited him at Cambridge in
the summer of 1912, when he had been there less than a
year, Russell told her: 'We expect the next big step in philosophy to be taken by your brother.'

As Russell's remark suggests, Wittgenstein was not following a conventional undergraduate course in philosophy. He
attended Russell's lectures, and, occasionally, those by Moore
and the other Cambridge philosophers, but there is nothing to
indicate that he ever seriously considered sitting any exami-
nations. His formal status was that of an undergraduate, but he

regarded himself, and, more remarkably, was regarded by others, not as a student of philosophy but as an original philosopher, attempting to provide new solutions to problems that were at the very cutting edge of the discipline.

It is possible, I think, that Cambridge is the only university in the world that would have accepted Wittgenstein on these terms. Had he broken off his engineering studies in order to study philosophy at Oxford, Vienna, Berlin, Paris, Harvard or any other leading university of the time, he would have fallen at the first hurdle, most likely rejected because of his almost complete ignorance of the work of any philosophers other than Frege and Russell. And, even if he had overcome this hurdle, he would have been obliged to do what, in fact, he never did throughout his entire life, namely study the works of the great philosophers of the past. Only after he had shown some understanding of Plato, Aristotle, Descartes, Leibniz, Hume, etc. would he have been allowed, as a graduate student, to devote himself to his own research.

At Cambridge, to its great credit, all that was required of Wittgenstein in order for him to reach this last stage – the stage at which he spent his time trying to solve philosophical problems rather than learning how previous philosophers had tried to solve them – was that he arouse the interest and admiration of Bertrand Russell. This he did in the Michaelmas (autumn) term of 1911, when, without any prior warning, he arrived at Russell's lectures to hear him speak and to argue with him about logic. In deciding whether or not to take on this eccentric young Austrian as a student, Russell did not ask Wittgenstein what he knew about the works of the great philosophers of the past; he asked him to write something about a philosophical problem that interested him. What Wittgenstein wrote is lost to history, but it was enough to convince Russell that Wittgenstein was serious and interesting, and six months later, he was looking to Wittgenstein to make the next big step in philosophy.

Wittgenstein's review of Coffey's *The Science of Logic* was written at a transitional stage in the relationship between him and Russell. During his first year at Cambridge, Wittgenstein had become Russell's favourite student, the one of whom he had the greatest expectations. In 1913, however, Russell stopped treating Wittgenstein as a student altogether, and began to defer to him on points of logic. In the summer of that year, a few months after this review was written, Russell's deferential attitude towards Wittgenstein was to have devastating repercussions on Russell's own intellectual development, when, after Wittgenstein criticized with great severity a draft of a book that he was working on, Russell became convinced, temporarily at least, that he had nothing further to contribute to fundamental questions in philosophy.

And yet, for all that, the review, more than anything else that Wittgenstein ever wrote, bears the mark of having been written by a disciple of Russell's. Because of the tensions in their relationship, both intellectual and personal, that developed in subsequent years, it is customary to emphasize the disagreements between Wittgenstein and Russell and to forget – what this review shows with great clarity – that Wittgenstein was at one time not only an adherent of Russell's ideas, but a fiercely partisan champion of them. In this way, the review, though admittedly a short and slight work of no great significance in itself, provides a good introduction to Wittgenstein's work, one that both provides the intellectual context of his thinking about logic and helps one to avoid the exegetical mistake of thinking that Wittgenstein's work should always be seen *in contrast* to Russell's work. What we see in this review is Wittgenstein fighting, with all the considerable polemical force at his disposal, *on the same side* as Russell.

The target of Wittgenstein's polemic, the unfortunate Professor P. Coffey, is a forgotten figure, obscure during his day and now known for nothing other than being the author of a book distinguished only for the extreme hostility with which it was reviewed by Wittgenstein. Coffey was an Irish Catholic, who announces himself in the preface to *The Science of Logic* to be a defender of the superiority of the Aristotelian/Scholastic system of logic over what he calls 'other systems now actually in vogue'. It is possible that he is here alluding to the 'new logic' of Frege and Russell, though in fact he never once mentions either (hence Wittgenstein's accusation that he 'has not taken the slightest notice of the great work of the modern mathematical logicians'). More likely, he is thinking of the various systems of logic developed by Keynes, Venn, De Morgan, Jevons, Mill and Whewell, all of whom he *does* discuss in the course of his defence of the Aristotelian system. Whatever, and whoever, he was defending Aristotle's logic against, his defence has won very few admirers and even fewer adherents.

In a review in *Mind* – the leading British journal of philosophy, which one might regard as representative of the British philosophical establishment – Coffey's book was criticized for being 'aggressively theological', and, even in 1913, it would have struck most logicians and philosophers as almost quaintly old-fashioned. It is clear from Wittgenstein's review, however, that he was not especially interested in the book itself ('only as a typical example of the work of many logicians today does this book deserve consideration'); what interests him, rather, is the opportunity presented by the review to state his conviction that the work on logic done by Frege and Russell represents a huge advance over the traditional Aristotelian system, an advance 'comparable only to that which made Astronomy out of Astrology, and Chemistry out of Alchemy'.

This is a very large claim, not only in its praise of modern mathematical logic but also in its denigration of Aristotle's logic, which is, after all, usually considered one of the greatest intellectual monuments of Western civilization. For over two thousand years, the logic taught and studied at academies, universities and monasteries was, essentially, that devised by Aristotle. The only contribution to science and culture that comes close to it in the longevity of its dominance is Euclid's system of geometry, which ruled the field from the sixth century BC until the development of non-Euclidean geometries in the middle of the nineteenth century. The reign of Aristotle's logic lasted slightly longer, coming to an end during the first decade of the twentieth century – just when Wittgenstein decided his future lay in philosophy rather than in engineering.

Like King Canute, Coffey, in defending Aristotle's logic against the modern mathematical barbarian hordes, was trying to hold back an inexorable tide, a tide that has wider cultural implications than might at first be apparent. Coffey, like most experts on Aristotle's logic, was not a scientist or a mathematician; he was a classicist, a man trained in Latin and Greek with little or no scientific education. The men against whom Coffey was defending Aristotle – Keynes, Venn, De Morgan, Jevons, Mill and Whewell – were either scientists or men with a scientific education. The final demise of Aristotelian logic marks the point at which logic as a discipline was taken out of the hands of classically trained scholars and put in those of mathematicians. Every significant advance in logic made in the twentieth century was made by someone with a mathematical background, and yet before the twentieth century logic was the preserve of the gentleman scholars. 'The worst of such books as this is that they prejudice sensible people against the study of Logic', says Wittgenstein in the conclusion to his review. What he means by 'sensible people', I think, is those with a scientific education. His point is that, so long as people like Coffey can get away with publishing books on 'The Science of Logic', logic will be avoided by genuine scientists.

If one wants to understand why Russell encouraged Wittgenstein's philosophical ambitions even though Wittgenstein was, from a conventional point of view, woefully under-educated in philosophy, it helps to think of the wider cultural struggle played out in Wittgenstein's review of Coffey. Russell had been, for some time before he met Wittgenstein, an advocate of what he called 'scientific method in philosophy'. His view was that progress in philosophy would be made by the kind of 'exact thinking' that had driven progress in mathematics and physics, and that, therefore, philosophy would do well to recruit students with some mathematical ability rather than those trained in the classics. When he met Wittgenstein, a man with a scientific education and a passionate interest in mathematical logic, he thought he had discovered his ideal. As he put it in a letter to his lover, Ottoline Morrell:

I believe a certain sort of mathematicians have far more philosophical capacity than most people who take up philosophy. Hitherto the people attracted to philosophy have been mostly those who loved the big generalizations, which were all wrong, so that few people with exact minds have taken up the subject. It has long been one of my dreams to found a great school of mathematically minded philosophers, but I don't know whether I shall ever get it accomplished. I had hopes of Norton, but he has not the physique, Broad is all right, but has no fundamental originality. Wittgenstein of course is exactly my dream.

In the years to come, Wittgenstein would surprise and disappoint Russell by his vehement rejection of what Russell called 'the scientific outlook', but in 1913 it looked as if Wittgenstein might well be the able lieutenant Russell was looking for in his campaign to inject some scientific rigour into the study of philosophy.

Certainly, Wittgenstein shows Coffey – and the entire scholarly tradition he seeks to defend – no mercy in this extraordinarily vitriolic, self-confident and didactic review. In place of a careful consideration of the merits and demerits of Coffey's book, Wittgenstein presents Coffey as representative of an intellectually lazy and outmoded approach to logic, one that feels able, in the name of Aristotle, to 'disregard the results of honest research' and, consequently, to repeat what 'the great work of the modern mathematical logicians' had shown were 'grave mistakes'.

All six of the 'mistakes' which Wittgenstein accuses Coffey of making involve ignoring aspects of the work of Frege and Russell. The first one ('The author believes that all propositions are of the subject–predicate form') raises an issue that had, for a long time, been close to Russell's heart. At the very beginning of his 1900 book on Leibniz, Russell had announced: 'That all sound philosophy should begin with an analysis of propositions is a truth too evident, perhaps, to demand a proof.' Russell's theme throughout the book is that Leibniz's mistaken views about metaphysics can be traced to a mistaken assumption about propositions, namely the very one of which Wittgenstein accuses Coffey: that every proposition has a subject and a predicate. The assumption that all propositions are of the subject–predicate form leads, Russell thought, to the belief that all *truths* are of that form, which, in turn, leads one to imagine the world as consisting of only two kinds of 'thing': objects (which correspond to subjects) and properties (which correspond to predicates).

It was of enormous philosophical importance, Russell believed, to acknowledge that, as well as objects and properties, the world contained *relations*. Propositions such as 'John is taller than his father' and 'Four is the square root of sixteen' must be understood, not as the predication of a property to an object, but as the assertion of a relation between two objects. But, to understand them as such requires one to break out of the subject–predicate straitjacket imposed upon propositions by Aristotelian logic. The logic of Frege and Russell, which treats propositions as *functions,* achieves this breakthrough. The word 'function' here is used with a conscious allusion to its origins in mathematics. Thus, just as the mathematical function x^2 has the value 16 when $x = 4$, and 25 when $x = 5$, so the *propositional function* 'x is taller than y' has the 'truth value' *true* when $x = $ John and $y = $ his father and *false* when $x = $ his father and $y = $ John.

Related to the notion of a propositional function is the notion – central to the logic developed by Frege and Russell – of a *class*. A class is the extension of a propositional function: i.e., it is the collection of things that, when given as the value(s) of the variable(s) in the function, result in a true proposition. For example, the function 'x is a man' has, as its extension, the class of men. The 'mistakes' IV, V and VI that Wittgenstein accuses Coffey of making all involve misunderstanding the notion of class as that notion was used in the logic of Frege and Russell. Of the others, II is a mistake only if the kind of philosophical realism espoused by Frege and Russell happens to be true, and III (the confusion between the two uses of the word 'is') raises again a point close to Russell's philosophical heart and one that he repeatedly invoked in arguing for the superiority of modern mathematical logic over the logic of Aristotle.

All in all, then, the review shows Wittgenstein at the very beginning of his philosophical career to be a particularly belligerent and partisan champion of the logic of Frege and Russell. It also reflects views about philosophy that remained characteristic of Wittgenstein's work throughout his life.

In the first place, it shows that, like Frege and Russell before him, he took logic to lie at the very heart of philosophy. Indeed, for him, philosophy simply *was* the attempt to understand logic. Secondly, it shows how seriously Wittgenstein took the view that the work of Frege and Russell *superseded* previous work in logic (and therefore in philosophy), to the extent that this previous work was simply not worth reading and considering. Wittgenstein often revealed (or perhaps 'boasted' is the word) to friends that he had never read a word of Aristotle. Evidently, he felt that he did not need to. If the work of Frege and Russell had indeed brought about an advance in Logic comparable to that which made Astronomy out of Astrology, and Chemistry out of Alchemy, then Aristotle's work – like that of, say, Descartes, Leibniz, Spinoza, Locke, Hume, Hegel and Mill (none of which Wittgenstein ever read) – was as obsolete as the works of the mediaeval alchemists.

In later life, Wittgenstein relaxed this attitude somewhat, and read with evident care and attention the work of, for example, Plato and Kant, but it remains true that no great philosopher has ever been so ignorant of the history of his subject as Wittgenstein was. He did not have the kind of education in philosophy that almost all other philosophers have had and that many consider to be a prerequisite for having anything interesting to say on the subject. Right from the very start, Wittgenstein's attitude to philosophy was very different from that which prevails among professional philosophers in academic institutions. He did not think of philosophy primarily as an academic subject, still less as a profession. For him, philosophy was the activity of solving philosophical problems. He used to say that, just as his father had been a businessman, so he took a businesslike attitude to philosophy. He wanted to *clear up* philosophical problems, like a businessman clears his desk.

2

CLEARING UP PHILOSOPHY IN THREE WORDS

This book will perhaps only be understood by those who have themselves already thought the thoughts which are expressed in it – or similar thoughts. It is therefore not a text-book. Its object would be attained if it afforded pleasure to one who read it with understanding.

The book deals with the problems of philosophy and shows, I believe, that the method of formulating these problems rests on the misunderstanding of the logic of our language. Its whole meaning could be summed up somewhat as follows: What can be said at all can be said clearly; and whereof one cannot speak thereof one must be silent.

The book will, therefore, draw a limit to thinking, or rather – not to thinking, but to the expression of thoughts; for in order to draw a limit to thinking we should have to be able to think both sides of this limit (we should therefore have to be able to think what cannot be thought).

The limit can, therefore, only be drawn in language and what lies on the other side of the limit will be simply nonsense.

How far my efforts agree with those of other philosophers

I will not decide. Indeed what I have here written makes no claim to novelty in points of detail; and therefore I give no sources, because it is indifferent to me whether what I have thought has already been thought before me by another.

I will only mention that to the great works of Frege and the writings of my friend Bertrand Russell I owe in large measure the stimulation of my thoughts.

If this work has a value it consists in two things. First that in it thoughts are expressed, and this value will be the greater the better the thoughts are expressed. The more the nail has been hit on the head. —Here I am conscious that I have fallen far short of the possible. Simply because my powers are insufficient to cope with the task. —May others come and do it better.

On the other hand the *truth* of the thoughts communicated here seems to me unassailable and definitive. I am, therefore, of the opinion that the problems have in essentials been finally solved. And if I am not mistaken in this, then the value of this work secondly consists in the fact that it shows how little has been done when these problems have been solved.

Preface to Tractatus Logico-Philosophicus, 1921

In 1921, eight years after publishing his review of Coffey's *The Science of Logic,* Wittgenstein published his first and only book. As the preface makes clear, it was supposed to be the last word on philosophical problems, to bring philosophy to an end. (And, sure enough, when he had finished the book, Wittgenstein gave up philosophy, returning to it only when, six years after the *Tractatus* was published, he became convinced that it was not, after all, the final word on the subject.)

Russell had dreamed of founding a school of philosophers

trained in mathematics whose 'exact minds' would resist the temptations of the 'big generalizations', all of which were false. What Wittgenstein – the man Russell regarded as the embodiment of that dream – had produced was a book that sought to avoid, not only the 'big generalizations', but *any* answers to philosophical problems as they have traditionally been raised. Philosophy would be cleared up, its problems solved once and for all, not by providing new answers to old questions but by showing that those old questions were ill-formed and arose from nothing more than 'the misunderstanding of the logic of our language'.

Russell had shown – or attempted to show – that Leibniz's metaphysical views rested upon a mistaken understanding of the nature of propositions; Wittgenstein wanted to show that *all* philosophical views rested upon a mistaken understanding of the nature of propositions. Indeed, the very questions that philosophers asked rested upon such misunderstandings. To attempt to answer a philosophical question was already to make a 'grave mistake', of the kind that Coffey made in defending Aristotelian logic. What was required was a correct understanding of the logic of our language. Once one had *that*, philosophical questions would not arise, for one would be able to see that any temptation to ask, let alone to answer, a philosophical question arose from a confusion about the logic of our language. A line would be drawn between what was thinkable and what was not, between sense and nonsense, and the whole of philosophy as traditionally conceived would be seen to lie on the wrong side of that line. In this way, the 'big generalizations' would be shown to be not false, but nonsensical.

But wait. Isn't the view that all philosophical problems rest upon a misunderstanding of the logic of our language *itself* a 'big generalization'? And so must we regard *that* as nonsense? Wittgenstein alludes to this problem in the preface when he says:

> The book will, therefore, draw a limit to thinking, or rather – not to thinking, but to the expression of thoughts; for in order to draw a limit to thinking we should have to be able to think both sides of this limit (we should therefore have to be able to think what cannot be thought).
>
> The limit can, therefore, only be drawn in language and what lies on the other side of the limit will be simply non-sense.

But this way of putting the problem simply avoids the difficulty. He admits that to draw a limit to thinking we should have to pretend to think both sides of the limit and thus pretend to be able to think what cannot be thought, but he appears to deny that the same thing applies to the *expression* of thoughts. If we draw a limit *in language* to what can be expressed and thus draw a line between sense and nonsense, what side of the limit does our 'line' – the expression of that limit – belong to? Just as, before, we had to think what cannot be thought, do we not now have to express what cannot be expressed?

In the body of the book, Wittgenstein deals directly with this problem and draws a surprising conclusion: that the book is an attempt to express what cannot be expressed, and, therefore, nonsense:

> My propositions serve as elucidations in the following way: anyone who understands me eventually recognizes them as nonsensical, when he has used them – as steps – to climb up beyond them. (He must, so to speak, throw away the

ladder after he has climbed up it.) He must transcend these propositions, and then he will see the world aright.

Thus, the view put forward in *Tractatus Logico-Philosophicus* appears to be that *all* philosophical propositions are nonsensical – including the ones in *Tractatus Logico-Philosophicus*. One is reminded of the first line of the *Tao Tê Ching*, which says: 'The Tao that can be expressed is not the eternal Tao.'

For Bertrand Russell, it came as something of a shock and a disappointment to discover that, when his favourite student, the very personification of his 'dream' of scientifically minded philosophers, finally produced a book, it had at its very heart a mystical paradox. In the introduction that he wrote to the book, Russell was fulsome in his praise of the book's achievements and of its significance. However, when he came to discuss Wittgenstein's apparent view that the truths of logic and philosophy (even those that were unassailable and definitive) are inexpressible, he demurred. 'What causes hesitation,' Russell wrote, 'is the fact that, after all, Mr Wittgenstein manages to say a good deal about what cannot be said.'

When Russell first read the book, two years before it was published, he sent Wittgenstein some questions about it. Somewhat reluctantly, Wittgenstein answered Russell's questions, but what he was most concerned to emphasize to Russell was the importance of the distinction between saying and showing:

Now I'm afraid you haven't really got hold of my main contention, to which the whole business of logical prop[osition]s is only a corollary. The main point is the theory of what can be expressed (gesagt) by prop[osition]s – i.e., by language – (and, which comes to the same, what can be

thought) and what cannot be expressed by prop[osition]s,
but only shown (gezeigt); which, I believe, is the cardinal
problem of philosophy.

In the *Tractatus* itself, Wittgenstein says: 'What *can* be shown,
cannot be said.'

Does this mean that Wittgenstein thought that the 'unassailable and definitive' truths that he claims in the preface to
be 'communicated' in the book are communicated by being
shown rather than said? This is how Russell interpreted him.
In his introduction, he says:

The whole subject of ethics, for example, is placed by
Mr Wittgenstein in the mystical, inexpressible region. Nevertheless he is capable of conveying his ethical opinions.
His defence would be that what he calls the mystical can
be shown, although it cannot be said. It may be that this
defence is adequate, but, for my part, I confess that it leaves
me with a certain sense of intellectual discomfort.

Frank Ramsey, the young Cambridge philosopher who had a
hand in the translation of the *Tractatus* and was one of its most
perceptive and enthusiastic admirers, put it more bluntly.
'What can't be said, can't be said,' Ramsey once remarked,
'and it can't be whistled either.'

More recently, strong doubts have been raised by interpreters of Wittgenstein about whether he *was* trying to
'whistle it', trying to *show* philosophical truths rather than to
state them. James Conant and Cora Diamond, two leading
Wittgenstein scholars, have developed a reading of the *Tractatus*
that tries to free it from the paradox that troubled Russell and
Ramsey. According to them, there is no way that one can

make sense of the book if one interprets Wittgenstein as believing that its propositions 1. express unassailable and definitive truths and 2. are nonsensical. Surely, they argue, a nonsensical proposition lacks *any* meaning, so it cannot possibly express a truth, unassailable or otherwise. Nonsense, according to them, can neither say nor show anything. They believe that the propositions in the *Tractatus* that look as if they are trying to express philosophical truths are indeed – and were intended by Wittgenstein to be – simply nonsensical. And, therefore, Conant and Diamond believe, these propositions do not say anything, and neither do they show anything.

However, the book, on their reading, still manages to communicate an unassailable and definitive truth about philosophy – viz., that any attempt to say something philosophical results in nonsense. It does this by getting the reader to see that its own propositions are nonsense and that they are nonsense *because* they try to say something philosophical. This interpretation offers an ingenious way round the paradox that lies at the heart of the 'standard' reading of the book. Unfortunately, it is extremely hard to square it with the text of the book itself and with other things that Wittgenstein said and wrote around the time that he wrote the book, things that seem to demonstrate that Wittgenstein did indeed believe that one could *show* deep truths, either by remaining silent about them or by saying things that, strictly speaking, were nonsensical.

Towards the end of *Tractatus Logico-Philosophicus*, Wittgenstein says: 'There is indeed the inexpressible. This *shows* itself; it is the mystical.' Among those things that 'show themselves' are ethics, aesthetics, religion, the meaning of life, logic and philosophy. In all these areas, Wittgenstein *appears* to believe, there are indeed truths, but none of these truths can be expressed in language; they all have to be shown, not said.

The distinction between what can be said and what can only be shown – what Wittgenstein, in his letter to Russell, calls the 'main point' of his book and the 'cardinal problem of philosophy' – was first made in writing by Wittgenstein in some notes on logic that he dictated to Moore in the spring of 1914. At that time, however, it was applied only to logic, not to ethics, aesthetics, religion and the meaning of life. So what Wittgenstein describes to Russell as 'only a corollary' to his main point was, in fact, the origin of the distinction. The extension of the distinction to these other areas occurred to Wittgenstein about two years later, when, while fighting for the Austrian army on the Russian Front, he continued to work on his book.

Wittgenstein's conception of the book he was writing changed considerably during the First World War. Before the war, he considered himself to be preparing a work on logic; after it, he considered himself to have written a book, the central point of which was fundamentally *ethical*. In a letter to a prospective publisher, Ludwig von Ficker, Wittgenstein warned that the book was difficult to understand and that von Ficker would most probably not understand it because 'the content will be strange to you'. But, he added:

> In reality, it isn't strange to you, for the point of the book is ethical. I once wanted to give a few words in the foreword which now are actually not in it, which, however, I'll write to you now because they might be a key for you: I wanted to write that my work consists of two parts: of the one which is here, and of everything which I have *not* written. And precisely this second part is the important one. For the Ethical is delimited from within, as it were, by my book;

and I'm convinced that, *strictly* speaking, it can ONLY be delimited in this way. In brief, I think: All of that which *many* are *babbling* today, I have defined in my book by remaining silent about it. Therefore the book will, unless I'm quite wrong, have much to say which you want to say yourself, but perhaps you won't notice that it is said in it. For the time being, I'd recommend that you read the *foreword* and the *conclusion* since these express the point most directly.

This seems to connect with Wittgenstein's remarks to Russell about the 'main point' of the book. Its main point is to answer the 'cardinal problem of philosophy', i.e., the question of where the limits of expressibility lie. In giving what he thought was a definitively and unassailably true answer to that question, Wittgenstein considered himself to have cleared up *all* problems of philosophy, and, in particular, to have defined the realm of the ethical. In both logic and ethics, the central point is the same and can be summed up in the sentence that occurs twice in the book, once in the preface and again as the final sentence: 'Whereof one cannot speak thereof one must be silent.'

In its final form, then, *Tractatus Logico-Philosophicus* is a curious hybrid of a book, a treatise on logic *and* the expression of a deeply mystical point of view. At the end of 1919, Russell, who had not seen Wittgenstein for six years, spent a week in Holland with him in order to go through the *Tractatus* line by line. He was shocked at the transformation in his 'dream' student brought about by his experiences in the war. 'I had felt in his book a flavour of mysticism', he wrote to Ottoline Morrell:

... but was astonished when I found he has become a complete mystic. He reads people like Kierkegaard and Angelus Silesius, and he seriously contemplates becoming a monk. It all started from William James's *Varieties of Religious Experience*, and grew (not unnaturally) during the winter he spent alone in Norway before the war, when he was nearly mad. Then during the war a curious thing happened. He went on duty to the town of Tarnov in Galicia, and happened to come upon a bookshop, which, however, seemed to contain nothing but picture postcards. However, he went inside and found that it contained just one book: Tolstoy on the Gospels. He bought it merely because there was no other. He read it and re-read it, and thenceforth had it always with him, under fire and at all times. But on the whole he likes Tolstoy less than Dostoewski (especially *Karamazov*). He has penetrated deep into mystical ways of thought and feeling, but I think (though he wouldn't agree) that what he likes best in mysticism is its power to make him stop thinking.

During the war, at the very time that his work was broadening out from logic to ethics, religion and the meaning of life, Wittgenstein made a close friend who was as sympathetic to and enthusiastic about Wittgenstein's mysticism as Russell had been earlier about his logic. His name was Paul Engelmann. After Wittgenstein's death, Engelmann published his correspondence with Wittgenstein, together with a memoir. His motive in publishing these things was to encourage a reading of the *Tractatus* that gave as much, or more, weight to its mysticism as to its theory of logic. About Russell's introduction to the book, Engelmann wrote: '[It] may be considered one of the main reasons why the book, though recognized to this day as an event of decisive importance in the field of logic, has failed to make itself understood as a philosophical work in the wider sense.'

Wittgenstein's correspondence with Engelmann does indeed help one to understand his mysticism. For example, in April 1917, Engelmann sent Wittgenstein a poem by Uhland called 'Count Eberhard's Hawthorn', which, very simply and without any embellishment, drawing of morals or even comment, tells the story of a soldier who, while on crusade, cuts a spray from a hawthorn bush, which, when he returns home, he plants in his garden. In old age, he sits beneath the shade of the fully grown hawthorn tree, which serves as a reminder of his youth. 'Almost all other poems,' Engelmann wrote to Wittgenstein, 'attempt to express the inexpressible; here that is not attempted, and precisely because of that it is achieved'.

Wittgenstein agreed. The poem, he said, was 'really magnificent . . . And this is how it is: if only you do not try to utter what is unutterable then *nothing* gets lost. But the unutterable will be – unutterably – *contained* in what has been uttered!'

This clearly became Wittgenstein's ideal: to communicate the inexpressible by *not* attempting to express it. At the end of the *Tractatus*, in between the two remarks already quoted – one to the effect that the inexpressible *shows* itself and the other to the effect that the propositions in the *Tractatus* are nonsense and to be treated like a ladder which one kicks away after one has used it – is the following remark about how, strictly speaking, philosophy *ought* to be done:

> The right method of philosophy would be this. To say nothing except what can be said, i.e., the propositions of natural science, i.e., something that has nothing to do with

> philosophy: and then always, when someone else wished to say something metaphysical, to demonstrate to him that he had given no meaning to certain signs in his propositions. This method would be unsatisfying to the other – he would not have the feeling that we were teaching him philosophy – but it would be the only strictly correct method.

It would seem to follow from this that, if one followed 'the right method of philosophy', then it would simply be impossible to write a book of philosophy. Such a book would be like the second part of the *Tractatus* as described by Wittgenstein to von Ficker, the 'important part' consisting of everything he had *not* written. It would, in other words, not exist. The 'first part' of the book, however, the part he *did* write, clearly does *not* conform to what he describes here as the right method of philosophy. Are we to regard him, then, as just straightforwardly inconsistent about how (and whether) philosophy should be written?

Is Wittgenstein, in other words, compromising his ideal when he writes *anything* in philosophy? If philosophy, like logic and ethics, belongs to the inexpressible, should he not conform to the advice given twice in the book and remain silent about it? The motto Wittgenstein chose for the book is a quotation from the poet Kürnberger: '. . . and anything a man knows, anything he has not merely heard rumbling and roaring, can be said in three words'. But, in the case of the inexpressible, surely, even three words are too many. Should we not, *must* we not, refrain from using any words at all?

Well, the poem by Uhland that was so admired by Engelmann and Wittgenstein does, after all, contain *some* words. Only those words are not *about* the meaning of life; they are about Count Eberhard and his hawthorn tree. And yet, Engelmann and Wittgenstein appeared to believe, precisely because nothing directly was said in the poem about its deeper meaning, that it managed to convey an inexpressible truth about the nature of life. Wittgenstein once wrote: 'I think I summed up my attitude to philosophy when I said: philosophy ought really to be written only as a *poetic composition*.' His admiration for Uhland's poem, I think, gives us a clue as to what he had in mind. If philosophical understanding is to be conveyed, then it cannot be in the same way that scientific knowledge is conveyed – i.e., stated directly in literal language – it must be through something more analogous to poetry. The philosopher has to bear in mind always that what he or she really wants to say cannot be said, and, therefore, it has be conveyed another way: it has to be *shown*. In this way, as Wittgenstein put it to Engelmann, the unutterable will be, unutterably, contained in what has been uttered.

But the mystery at the heart of the *Tractatus* (as the book is traditionally read) is deeper than this would suggest. For, after all, though the sentences in Uhland's poem are not *about* the meaning of life (but about the planting and growth of a hawthorn tree), neither are they complete nonsense. In this way they are crucially different from the sentences which make up the *Tractatus*, which, Wittgenstein says, should be recognized as nonsense by anyone who understands him. This, I think, is where adherents of the Conant–Diamond interpretation are on their strongest ground. It is one thing to say that the sentences of Uhland's poem show something in addition to what they say; it is quite another to claim that the sentences of the *Tractatus* succeed in showing something even though, being nonsensical, they fail to say *anything*. It would be much easier to understand Wittgenstein's distinction between saying and showing if it applied only to meaningful propositions. We could still then make sense of his admiration for Uhland's poem and of his remark that philosophy ought to be written as a poetic composition (after all, the difference between a poetic composition and a scientific one is not that the former is nonsense), but we would not be saddled with the extremely problematic view that important truths can be shown by sentences that lack any meaning at all.

However, there are clear signs in the *Tractatus* that Wittgenstein does indeed think that nonsense can, at least sometimes, *show* something than cannot be said. Take, for example, what he says about ethics. On the one hand, he says: 'there can be no ethical propositions . . . It is clear that ethics cannot be expressed. Ethics is transcendental.' On the other hand, on the very same page in the book, he states:

> . . . it is clear that ethics has nothing to do with punishment and reward in the ordinary sense. The question as to the *consequences* of an action must therefore be irrelevant. At least these consequences will not be events. For there must be something right in that formulation of the question. There must be some sort of ethical reward and ethical punishment, but this must lie in the action itself.
>
> (And this is clear also that the reward must be something acceptable, and the punishment something unacceptable.)

If these are not intended to be 'ethical propositions', what are they supposed to be? Granted they are not ethical propositions in the sense that, for example, the sentence 'It was morally wrong to go to war with Iraq' is an ethical proposition, but they *are* propositions that seem to be *about* ethics, propositions that attempt to characterize ethics. And is not the characterization of ethics one of the things that has to be shown rather than said? In his letter to von Ficker, Wittgenstein wrote, apropos of the ethical purpose of the book: 'All of that which *many* are *babbling* today, I have defined in my book by remaining silent about it.' But in the passage above, he is *not* silent about ethics; he states, quite directly, a particular, anti-consequentialist, view of ethics, one that contradicts, for example, utilitarianism. If ethics and philosophy are both 'transcendental', if both belong to the realm of the inexpressible, then surely, *a fortiori*, a philosophical view *about* ethics should be inexpressible. So, the sentences above *must be*, according to Wittgenstein, nonsensical, as indeed he draws to the reader's attention when he says that 'he who understands me finally recognizes them [the propositions in his book] as nonsense'. But, *contra* Conant and Diamond, it is clear, I think, that Wittgenstein believes that what the propositions above are *trying* to say is indeed true. He does indeed, for example, believe that: 'ethics has nothing to do with punishment and reward in the ordinary sense', but he also believes that, strictly speaking, this ethical truth cannot be stated but has to be shown. It would seem to be Wittgenstein's view, then, that one of the ways in which things that cannot be expressed can be shown is through the failed attempt to express them; in other words, that nonsensical propositions – his own, for example – can indeed show what they fail to say.

The ongoing debate about the saying/showing distinction and about whether or not Wittgenstein thought it was possible to show philosophical truths through nonsensical propositions is just one among many controversies that divide interpreters of *Tractatus Logico-Philosophicus*. And these controversies do not concern details but the very fundamentals of the book. More than eighty years after it was published, and despite a vast secondary literature inspired by it, there is still no general agreement about how the book should be read. It is surely one of the most enigmatic pieces of philosophy ever published: too mystical for logicians, too technical for mystics, too poetic for philosophers and too philosophical for poets, it is a work that makes extraordinarily few concessions to the reader and seems consciously designed to elude comprehension.

Wittgenstein says in the preface that the purpose of the book would be achieved 'if it afforded pleasure to one who read it with understanding'. With this in mind, it is interesting and revealing to see *who* in particular he hoped and expected would understand it.

The final version of the book was completed during leave from active service in the summer of 1918. As soon as it was finished, he sent it to the publisher Jahoda. This is an interesting choice because Jahoda was not an academic publisher but a literary one, best known as the publisher of the Viennese satirist Karl Kraus. In the 1930s, Wittgenstein listed Kraus, along with more predictable names like Frege and Russell, as one of the people who had most influenced his work. Although he is not very well known in the English-speaking world, Kraus was enormously influential among the Viennese intellectual and social elite of Wittgenstein's generation. He was the editor – and, for the most part, the writer – of the journal *Die Fackel* (The Torch), which was launched in 1899 and quickly became required reading for the younger generation of artists and intellectuals in Vienna, who formed a reverential admiration for the devastatingly witty and acerbic way in which Kraus mocked the hypocrisy of the Habsburg Establishment.

In sending the book to Jahoda, it seems, Wittgenstein was hoping that it would be sent to Kraus and that Kraus would recognize Wittgenstein as an ally in his campaign for decency, clarity and integrity in Austrian life. In other words, he was hoping that Kraus would understand what he told von Ficker he had once wanted to spell out in the preface: the unspoken, but centrally important, ethical purpose of the book. Perhaps he even hoped that in *Tractatus Logico-Philosophicus* Kraus would see that his own ethical point of view had received its definitive expression, and recognize the intellectual and moral superiority of *this* expression over the 'babbling' that prevailed in literary and artistic circles.

However, if Wittgenstein was hoping that Kraus would understand this, he was to be disappointed. About a month after he returned from leave, he received a letter from Jahoda saying that they would not publish the book 'for technical reasons'. Writing to Engelmann about this rejection – the first of many – Wittgenstein remarked: 'I would dearly like to know what Kraus said about it.'

In all probability, if Kraus was ever shown the book by Jahoda, the chances are that he would not have made any sense of it whatsoever. What Wittgenstein regarded as the book's central point – that the most important truths (of ethics, aesthetics and religion) were those about which we are forced to be silent – was familiar enough to Kraus, but Wittgenstein's way of demonstrating that point – through an analysis of the problems about the nature of logic that dogged the work of Frege and Russell – would have been entirely alien to him.

But, if the book was too technical for Kraus, it was too poetic for the other person whom Wittgenstein hoped and expected to understand it: Gottlob Frege. Frege was by this time, at seventy years old, a fairly elderly man, whose mind was still precise but not, perhaps, as flexible as it had once been. It took Frege a long time to respond to the book, and, by the time he wrote to Wittgenstein about it in June 1919, Wittgenstein had been an Italian prisoner-of-war for seven months. Frege's response consisted entirely of requests for clarification, asking Wittgenstein what he meant by this or that word or phrase. When Wittgenstein replied to these questions as best he could, Frege came back wanting more explanations, telling Wittgenstein that he would be unable to recommend the book to a publisher because 'the content is too unclear to me'. In any case, Frege was worried about the first sentence of Wittgenstein's preface, about the idea that the book would be understood only by those who had the same, or similar thoughts. If this were so, Frege told Wittgenstein: 'The pleasure of reading your book can therefore no longer be aroused by the content which is already known, but only by the peculiar form given to it by the author. The book thereby becomes an artistic rather than a scientific achievement; what is said in it takes second place to the way in which it is said.' After receiving this letter, Wittgenstein abandoned any hope of getting Frege to understand the book.

Only after he had received these disheartening responses from Kraus and Frege did Wittgenstein send a copy of the *Tractatus* to Russell, having previously told him that he would not understand it without explanation. Having received Frege's second letter about the book, Wittgenstein wrote to Russell that Frege 'doesn't understand a word of it . . . So my only hope is to see *you* soon and explain all to you, for it is VERY hard not to be understood by a single soul!'

The week in Holland that Russell and Wittgenstein spent together at the end of 1919 was devoted to a line-by-line explanation of the book, after which both considered that Russell understood the book sufficiently to write an introduction to it. However, when Wittgenstein received Russell's introduction, he was unhappy with it. 'There's so much of it that I'm not in agreement with,' he told Russell, 'both where you're critical of me and also where you're simply trying to elucidate my point of view.' After Russell's introduction had been translated into German, Wittgenstein could not bring himself to agree to its publication. 'All the refinement of your English style was, obviously, lost in the translation,' he wrote to Russell, adding cuttingly, 'and what remained was superficiality and misunderstanding.' *Tractatus Logico-Philosophicus* was eventually published eighteen months later, and only because Wittgenstein relented on the inclusion of Russell's introduction (without which no publisher would touch it). There is nothing to indicate, however, that he ever considered Russell's introduction to contain anything other than superficiality, misunderstanding and, in its original English, a refined style.

'Its purpose would be achieved if it gave pleasure to one person who read and understood it.' At the time of its publication, despite being sent to the three people Wittgenstein thought most likely to understand it, it was an open question whether, by this measure, its purpose had been achieved or not. Eighty years later, it is still an open question.

3

PICTURING THE WORLD

1.   The world is everything that is the case.
1.1.   The world is the totality of facts, not of things.
1.11. The world is determined by the facts, and by these
       being *all* the facts.
1.12. For the totality of facts determines both what is the
       case, and also all that is not the case.
1.13. The facts in logical space are the world.
1.2.   The world divides into facts.
1.21. Any one can either be the case or not be the case,
       and everything else remain the same.

Tractatus Logico-Philosophicus, 1921

One reason that *Tractatus Logico-Philosophicus* is such a difficult work is the utter weirdness of its style. Nothing before or since, in philosophy, science or literature, has been written quite like it. The book begins with the seven numbered propositions quoted above. The numbers are off-putting and disorientating. When von Ficker was considering whether to publish the book, he asked Wittgenstein plaintively if the numbers were absolutely necessary. Yes, they were, Wittgenstein replied, 'because they alone give the book lucidity and clarity and it would be an incomprehensible jumble without them'.

The one concession Wittgenstein makes to the reader is a footnote to the very first proposition, in which he explains the significance of the numbers: 'The decimal numbers assigned to the individual propositions indicate the logical importance of the propositions, the stress laid on them in my exposition. The propositions $n.1$, $n.2$, $n.3$, etc., are comments on proposition no. n; the propositions $n.m1$, $n.m2$, etc. are comments on proposition no. $n.m$; and so on.' So, for example, proposition 1.1 is a comment on proposition 1 and proposition 1.11 is a comment on proposition 1.1.

Though strange and unfamiliar, the basic idea of the numbering is not difficult to grasp. What *is* difficult to understand is what Wittgenstein is trying to say with these oracular pronouncements and how they are supposed to help in providing what was promised in the preface: a solution to all the problems of philosophy.

To understand *that*, it helps to have some idea of the structure of the book, as that structure is indicated by Wittgenstein's number scheme. If we take Wittgenstein at his word about the significance of the numbers, then there are only seven propositions that are *not* comments on other propositions, and these, we must assume, are those that he regards as the most logically important. They are:

1. The world is all that is the case.
2. What is the case – a fact – is the existence of states of affairs.
3. A logical picture of facts is a thought.
4. A thought is a proposition with a sense.
5. A proposition is a truth-function of elementary propositions.

(An elementary proposition is a truth-function of itself.)

6. The general form of a truth-function is $[\bar{p}, \bar{\xi}, N(\bar{\xi})]$.
    This is the general form of a proposition.

7. Whereof one cannot speak, thereof one must be silent.

Leaving aside for the moment the fact that almost all of these propositions are, without considerable help, completely unintelligible, there *is* a discernible structure here: the book tells us first what the world is, then what a fact is, then what a thought is, and then, at much greater length (propositions 4, 5 and 6 are all devoted to this), what a proposition is. Finally, it tells us – what in the preface had been described as the 'whole meaning' of the book – that we have to remain silent about that which we cannot speak.

How much greater the section on propositions is than the others is somewhat disguised by this bare structure. For, though each of these seven propositions is accorded the same logical significance, they do not receive equal amounts of 'commentary'. Proposition 7, for example, stands entirely alone. It is the very last sentence of the book; there is no proposition 7.1. Proposition 1 has a mere six 'sub-propositions' (all quoted above) taking up less than half a page. Of the others, proposition 2 has five pages of commentary, 3 eight pages, 4 eighteen pages, 5 twenty-two pages and 6 fifteen pages. The notion of a proposition is introduced at 3.1, so that of the eight pages of commentary devoted to proposition 3 (which, ostensibly, is about thought), seven of them are about propositions. The bulk of the book, then, something like 90% of it, is concerned with the nature of the proposition.

Though Wittgenstein's remarks about the world, facts and thoughts appear in the book *before* his discussion of propositions, it is clear that the logical priority is the other way round. What Wittgenstein says about these other things depends upon, and only makes sense in the light of, what he says about propositions. Indeed, Wittgenstein's claim that the book clears up the whole of philosophy turns out to rest upon his belief that the whole of philosophy amounts to a single question: what is a proposition? This, in turn, sheds light on what he means when he says that the way philosophical problems had previously been formulated rests on 'the misunderstanding of the logic of our language', and also on what he means when he remarks how little is achieved when philosophical problems are solved. To give an unassailably true and definitive answer to the question 'what is a proposition?' may seem a small achievement – and Wittgenstein would agree that it is. On the other hand, in doing so, Wittgenstein would claim, one has, for what it is worth, solved *all* the problems of philosophy.

Before we get to Wittgenstein's analysis of propositions, however, we have short sections on the world, facts and thought. One might think that the world is quite a big subject, but Wittgenstein's section discussing it is particularly brief. The entire world, so to speak, is disposed of in the seven propositions quoted above.

And yet, these seven propositions are as revolutionary as anything else in the book. If taken seriously, they lead to a conception of the world that removes at a single stroke a lot of traditional metaphysics. Think, for example, of Russell's objections to Leibniz: Leibniz was, Russell believed, trapped by the Aristotelian conception of a proposition into thinking of the world as consisting of objects and properties, while ignoring the fact that the world also contains relations. Russell argued this point also with his contemporary, the Oxford philosopher F. H. Bradley. Bradley argued that, if relations existed, we would have to think of them as a kind of object. But since they are clearly not a kind of object, they do not, after all, exist. Russell countered by accepting Bradley's initial premise (that, if relations existed, they would be a kind of object), but drawing the opposite conclusion. His argument was that, since relations clearly *do* exist, they must, indeed, be a kind of object.

Wittgenstein wanted to do away with all arguments of this kind (they are classic examples of what he described as nonsense). One of his original uses of the distinction between showing and saying was to try to convince Russell that the existence of objects, properties and relations was one of those things that had to be shown rather than stated. As he put it in the notes he dictated to Moore in 1914:

> This same distinction between what can be *shewn* by the language but not *said*, explains the difficulty that is felt about types – e.g., as to [the] difference between things, facts, properties, relations. That M is a *thing* can't be *said*; it is nonsense; but *something* is *shewn* by the symbol 'M'. In [the] same way, that a *proposition* is a subject-predicate proposition can't be said: but it is *shown* by the symbol.

The fact that our language has different types of words – words for things (objects), properties and relations – *shows* what Russell is trying to say when, in disagreeing with Leibniz and Bradley, he insists that relations are as real as objects and properties. Disputes like these cannot be settled by asserting facts about the world, Wittgenstein insisted; they are settled – they disappear – when we understand the roles played by different types of word in the construction of propositions. Any attempt to *say* what is *shown* about the world by, for example, a subject–predicate proposition or a relational proposition will result in nonsense.

When Russell and Wittgenstein met in Holland, they argued this point at particularly great length, Russell trying to persuade Wittgenstein that the sentence 'There are at least three things in the world' was both meaningful and true. Russell later recollected that during the discussion he took a sheet of white paper and made three blobs of ink on it, urging Wittgenstein to admit that, since there were three blobs, there must be at least three things in the world, 'but he refused resolutely . . . He would admit there were three blobs on the page, because that was a finite assertion, but he would not admit that anything at all could be said about the world as a whole.' That the world contains at least three things is shown by there being three blobs, but 'the world contains at least three things' is, for Wittgenstein, no more a meaningful proposition than 'the world contains objects, properties and relations'.

The first two propositions of the *Tractatus* are an attempt by Wittgenstein to conceive of the world in such a way as to make it obvious that nothing can be gained by arguing about the existence or otherwise of objects, properties and relations. We are to think of the world, not as made up of 'things' but as made up of *facts*. The crucial difference is that things are simple, but a fact is *articulate*, in the sense that an articulated lorry is articulate, i.e., it has *parts*. These parts are what Wittgenstein calls *objects*, but we can know nothing about objects *except* insofar as they constitute a fact. Facts are what correspond to (true) propositions (which is why what Wittgenstein means by 'The world is the totality of facts' cannot really be understood until one understands what a proposition is) and objects are what correspond to words. A word on its own means nothing. Words *refer* to objects but they *mean* something only insofar as they are part of a proposition. The smallest unit of meaningful language is not the word but the proposition (the exclamation 'Fire!' is not an exception to this, since it is an abbreviated proposition, being short for something like: 'There is a fire in this room!'). In this way, language is not made up of words, but of propositions, and, in the same way, the world is not made up of objects but of facts.

Of course, if, as Wittgenstein insisted to Russell, nothing can be said about the world as a whole, it follows that each of the seven propositions with which the *Tractatus* opens is an attempt to say something that cannot be said and is therefore meaningless. This much is explicitly acknowledged by Wittgenstein and is common ground among his interpreters. What the reader has to decide for him or herself, however, is this: does Wittgenstein nevertheless think that the things that these propositions are *trying* to say are true or is he offering them as the kind of nonsense that philosophers fall into when they try to use language beyond its limits? The traditional interpretation says the first; the Conant–Diamond interpretation says the second. I favour the traditional interpretation; it seems to me that Wittgenstein really does believe that, for example, the world is the totality of facts not of things, and he also believes that any attempt (including his own) to *say* this has to result in nonsense.

In any case, the very brevity of his discussion of the world seems to have a philosophical point, namely to suggest to Russell *et al*. that this is not where the real problems lie. Disputes about 'the world' arise, Wittgenstein believed, like all philosophical problems, from a misunderstanding of the logic of our language, and can therefore only be resolved through a correct analysis of propositions.

The way Wittgenstein gets from the world to where he thinks *all* the problems and answers really lie, i.e., the proposition, is via the notion of a *thought*.

Having urged us to think of the world as being made up of facts not of things, Wittgenstein then, at 2.1. introduces the central idea of *picturing* the facts of the world. 'We picture facts to ourselves,' he says, elaborating the idea in the following ways (in what follows some propositions have been omitted):

2.12.   A picture is a model of reality.

2.13.   In a picture objects have the elements of the picture corresponding to them.

2.131. In a picture the elements of the picture are the representatives of objects.

2.14.   What constitutes a picture is that its elements are related to one another in a determinate way.

2.141. A picture is a fact.

2.18.   What any picture, of whatever form, must have in common with reality, in order to be able to depict it – correctly or incorrectly – in any way at all, is logical form, i.e., the form of reality.

2.181. A picture whose pictorial form is logical form is called a logical picture.

2.182. Every picture is *at the same time* a logical one. (On the other hand, not every picture is, for example, a spatial one.)

3.   A logical picture of facts is a thought.

3.1.   In the proposition the thought is expressed perceptibly through the senses.

Here we can see how important it is to Wittgenstein's analysis that facts are articulate. It is because facts have parts that they can be pictured, the elements of the picture corresponding to the objects that constitute the fact. This idea came to Wittgenstein during the First World War when he read in a magazine a report of a court case in Paris concerning a car accident, in which a model of the accident was presented before the court. What struck Wittgenstein was that the model could represent the accident because of the correspondence between the parts of the model (the miniature houses, cars, people, etc.) and the real houses, cars, people, etc. In this way, 'the elements of the picture are the representatives of objects'.

The courtroom model was a *spatial* picture in that the spatial relations between the model figures represent the spatial relations between the cars, people, etc. in the real world. Each rearrangement of the elements of the model gives a different picture of how things stood at the time of accident. But, it is not necessary that in every picture the elements of the picture be *spatially* related, just that the picture *has* elements which can have *some* sort of relations to one another. For example, if a melody is held to represent a situation in the world (in the way, for example, that Beethoven's Sixth Symphony is held to represent a walk in the forest), then the representation cannot be achieved through *spatial* relations (how far the violinists stand from the wind section has nothing to do with it) but rather through temporal relations. Both temporal and spatial relations might provide the *form* of the picture, but whatever form the picture has, the fact that it has a form at all means that it has a *logical* form. *Any* picture of whatever form has a logical form, which is to say (given that 'a logical picture of facts is a thought') that every picture expresses a thought. A proposition is a thought expressed in a way that is perceptible by the senses. In other words, a proposition is a kind of picture.

Its meaning is the state of affairs pictured by it; the state of affairs might obtain in the real world or not. If it does, the proposition is true, if it does not the proposition is false. But, either way, the proposition pictures a *possible* state of affairs.

4

WHAT IS A PROPOSITION?

.

3. A logical picture of facts is a thought.

　. . .

3.1. In a proposition a thought finds an expression that can be perceived by the senses.

3.11. We use the perceptible sign of a proposition (spoken or written, etc.) as a projection of a possible situation.

　The method of projection is to think of the sense of the proposition.

3.12. I call the sign with which we express a thought a propositional sign. —And a proposition is a propositional sign in its projective relation to the world.

　. . .

3.14. What constitutes a propositional sign is that in it its elements (the words) stand in a determinate relation to one another.

　A propositional sign is a fact.

3.141. A proposition is not a blend of words. —(Just as a theme in music is not a blend of notes.)

　A proposition is articulate.

3.142. Only facts can express a sense, a set of names cannot.

3.143. Although a propositional sign is a fact, this is obscured by the usual form of expression in writing or print.

For in a printed proposition, for example, no essential difference is apparent between a propositional sign and a word.

3.1431. The essence of a propositional sign is very clearly seen if we imagine one composed of spatial objects (such as tables, chairs and books) instead of written signs.

Then the spatial arrangement of these things will express the sense of the proposition.

. . .

3.2. In a proposition a thought can be expressed in such a way that elements of the propositional sign correspond to the objects of the thought.

. . .

3.22. In a proposition a name is the representative of an object.

3.221. Objects can only be named. Signs are their representatives. I can only speak *about* them: I cannot *put them into words*. Propositions can only say *how* things are, not *what* they are.

. . .

3.25. A proposition has one and only one complete analysis.

. . .

3.3. Only propositions have sense; only in the nexus of a proposition does a name have meaning.

. . .

3.32. A sign is what can be perceived of a symbol.

3.321. So one and the same sign (written or spoken, etc.) can be common to two different symbols – in which case they will signify in different ways.

. . .

3.323. In everyday language it very frequently happens that the same word has different modes of signification – and so belongs to different symbols – or that two words that have different modes of signification are employed in propositions in what is superficially the same way.

Thus the word 'is' figures as the copula, as a sign for identity, and as an expression for existence; 'exist' figures as an intransitive verb like 'go', and 'identical' as an adjective; we speak of *something*, but also of *something's* happening.

(In the proposition, 'Green is green' – where the first word is the proper name of a person and the last an adjective – these words do not merely have different meanings: they are *different symbols*.)

3.324. In this way the most fundamental confusions are easily produced (the whole of philosophy is full of them).

3.325. In order to avoid such errors we must make use of a sign-language that excludes them by not using the same sign for different symbols and by not using in a superficially similar way signs that have different modes of signification: that is to say, a sign-language that is governed by *logical* grammars – by logical syntax.

(The conceptual notation of Frege and Russell is such a language, though, it is true, it fails to exclude all mistakes.)

. . .

4. A thought is a proposition with a sense.

4.001. The totality of propositions is language.

. . .

4.01. A proposition is a picture of reality.

A proposition is a model of reality as we imagine it.

4.011. At first sight a proposition – one set out on the printed page, for example – does not seem to be a picture of the reality with which it is concerned. But neither do written notes seem at first sight to be a picture of a piece of music, nor our phonetic notation (the alphabet) to be a picture of our speech.

And yet these sign-languages prove to be pictures, even in the ordinary sense, of what they represent.

Tractatus Logico-Philosophicus, 1921

In the early sections of *Tractatus Logico-Philosophicus*, Wittgenstein establishes that a *thought* is a picture of reality, a *logical* picture. A proposition, too, is a picture; indeed, a proposition is a thought that has found expression. In the above sections of the book, Wittgenstein distinguishes between *sign* and *symbol*. The propositional sign is the collection of marks on a piece of paper, sounds uttered by the mouth, etc. that constitute the spoken or written words used to express the thought. The sign, then, is something physical, something perceptible. The symbol is what is common to all signs that are used to express the same thought. It often happens that in everyday language the same sign is used to express very different thoughts; in which case, the two instances of the sign are actually different symbols. For example, in the sentence 'Green is green' (used, perhaps, to express the thought that somebody called John Green is jealous), the two instances of the sign 'green' are, despite appearances, different symbols.

In this and other ways, our everyday language disguises the underlying logical form of the thoughts it is used to express. Philosophy, Wittgenstein believes (see, e.g., 3.324 above), is, for the most part, a series of problems that have arisen because of the confusion caused by this disguise. In this way, it can often help in philosophy to re-express thoughts in the kind of artificial, formal languages invented by Frege and Russell. However, one must not be misled by this into thinking (a) that there is such a thing as a 'correct' sign-language or (b) that there is anything wrong with the language we have. The problem with our everyday language is not that it is inadequate to express our thoughts, nor that it stands in need of improvement in order to express thoughts more precisely (see 5.5563: '. . . all the propositions of our everyday language, just as they stand, are in perfect logical order'); the problem is that it does not, so to speak, wear its own logical form on its sleeve. This is a problem, not for ordinary language-users, but for philosophers, who tend not to notice that their questions are the result of not seeing clearly enough the logic of our language. So, for example, if you are aware that the word 'is' can be used to express predication ('Green is green') and identity ('Green is Green'), then no confusion need be caused. If you are not aware of this, then you will make the 'grave mistakes' made by philosophers such as Coffey.

Wittgenstein lays great stress on the thought that a proposition is a *fact*. Notice the curious – and surely deliberate – parallel between propositions 2.14/2.141 and 3.14/3.141:

> 2.14. What constitutes a picture is that its elements are related to one another in a determinate way.
> 2.141. A picture is a fact.
> 3.14. What constitutes a propositional sign is that in it its elements (the words) stand in a determinate relation to one another.
>   A propositional sign is a fact.
> 3.141. A proposition is not a blend of words. —(Just as a theme in music is not a blend of notes.)
>   A proposition is articulate.

'Only facts can express a sense, a set of names cannot' (3.142). It follows from this that: 'Only propositions have sense; only in the nexus of a proposition does a name have meaning'

(3.3). The model in the Paris courtroom that Wittgenstein read about becomes for him a way of seeing clearly the very *essence* of a proposition (see 3.1431 above). The reason the essence of a proposition is seen more clearly when we imagine one composed of spatial objects is that then its pictorial character becomes more obvious; we do not get misled by the fact that: 'At first sight a proposition – one set out on the printed page, for example – does not seem to be a picture.'

From the notion that a proposition is essentially a picture of reality, Wittgenstein goes on in the rest of the book to draw far-reaching conclusions about logic, about what can be said and what cannot, and about the nature of philosophy.

At the heart of all these far-reaching conclusions is the thought that to express a sense is to picture a portion of reality; therefore anything that does not picture a state of affairs is senseless. This includes all the so-called propositions of logic. Logic is the study of inferential relations between propositions, but, according to Wittgenstein, to say that one proposition can be inferred from, or that it follows from, other propositions, is just to say that these other propositions have already said whatever the inferred proposition says. For example, the reason that 'Socrates is mortal' follows from 'All men are mortal' and 'Socrates is a man' is that among the things said by these two latter propositions is that Socrates is mortal. So, the argument:

All men are mortal
Socrates is a man
Therefore Socrates is mortal

is, in fact, a tautology. Logic is not a science that discovers truths; it is just a collection of tautologies. And a tautology is *not* a picture of reality. 'It is either raining or it is not raining' is always true – it is, in Wittgenstein's sense, a tautology – but it is not a truth that tells you anything about the world. To know that it is either raining or not raining is not to know anything about the weather; it is just to know that that sentence embraces *every* possibility and that, therefore, it cannot possibly be false. To know that it is always true, therefore, is to know something about our language, not about our weather. Tautologies, according to Wittgenstein, are *senseless*, because, as they do not picture the world, they lack sense. However, they are not *nonsense*, because they are a legitimate part of our sign-language, just as the numeral for zero, 0, is part of the sign-language of mathematics, even though (quite literally) it signifies nothing.

Just as tautologies are always true, contradictions (e.g., 'It is raining and not raining') are always false, and, like tautologies, do not, therefore, picture anything in the world. If one thinks of an ordinary proposition as a photographic picture, then a tautology can be likened to a shot which is so over-exposed that everything is white, and a contradiction to a shot that is so under-exposed that everything is black. Wittgenstein calls tautologies and contradictions 'pseudo-propositions'; they are not real propositions, because real propositions can be *either* true or false.

A picture has to have *something* in common with what it pictures. This 'something' Wittgenstein calls 'pictorial form'; pictorial form can be spatial, temporal, etc., but it *has* to be *logical*. Everything in the world can be pictured, but a picture cannot represent its own pictorial form; that has to be shown rather than said. The form of our language – and, therefore, of the world – is shown by logic; logic, therefore, belongs to the unsayable. It is, as Wittgenstein puts it, 'transcendental' (see 6.13).

Every logical proposition, every tautology, is of equal value; there are no 'logical axioms' and no logical facts. The systems of logic built by Frege and Russell, therefore, assume a mistaken view of what logic is.

As we have seen, logic is not alone in being 'transcendental' in Wittgenstein's sense. Ethics, aesthetics and religion are also transcendental in this sense; that is, the 'truths' belonging to them cannot be stated in meaningful propositions. The reason for that is that meaningful propositions are limited to picturing states of affairs *in the world*, and value, whether ethical, aesthetic or religious, is not to be found in the world. In other words, there are no ethical *facts*. This is why there cannot be any ethical propositions

To understand the logic of our language, to see that logic, ethics, aesthetics and religion are transcendental is to appreciate what Wittgenstein calls the 'main point' of *Tractatus Logico-Philosophicus*. It is, in other words, to see the final, definitive and unassailably true solution to the problems of philosophy. And one of the things that becomes clear in this 'seeing' is what Wittgenstein claims has been misunderstood by almost all philosophers: namely, the nature of philosophy itself.

5

WHAT IS PHILOSOPHY?

4.11. The totality of true propositions is the whole of natural science (or the whole corpus of the natural sciences).

4.111. Philosophy is not one of the natural sciences.

(The word 'philosophy' must mean something whose place is above or below the natural sciences, not beside them.)

4.112. Philosophy aims at the logical clarification of thoughts.

Philosophy is not a body of doctrine but an activity.

A philosophical work consists essentially of elucidations.

Philosophy does not result in 'philosophical propositions', but rather in the clarification of propositions.

Without philosophy thoughts are, as it were, cloudy and indistinct: its task is to make them clear and to give them sharp boundaries.

4.1121. Psychology is no more closely related to philosophy than any other natural science.

Theory of knowledge is the philosophy of psychology.

Does not my study of sign-language correspond to the study of thought-processes, which philosophers used to consider so essential to the philosophy of logic? Only in most cases they got entangled in unessential psychological investigations, and with my method too there is an analogous risk.

4.1122. Darwin's theory has no more to do with philosophy than any other hypothesis in natural science.

4.113. Philosophy sets limits to the much disputed sphere of natural science.

Tractatus Logico-Philosophicus, 1921

The task of philosophy, as Wittgenstein sees it, is to reveal the true nature of the logic of our language, and thereby to 'solve' the philosophical problems that arise when that logic is misunderstood. The solving of philosophical problems in this way is best done on a case-by-case basis. Thus, philosophy is an activity, not a doctrine. It is the activity of 'the logical clarification of thoughts'. The *Tractatus* should not be seen as a book of philosophical propositions, for, strictly speaking, there are no such things. Rather, it should be seen as a set of 'elucidations' that should be regarded as transitory stages towards philosophical clarification. If one has achieved the clarity that the elucidations seek to impart, one will be able to see that the so-called propositions of the *Tractatus* are, in fact, nonsense.

In 1913, Russell had looked to Wittgenstein to take the next big step in philosophy, to solve the problems about the nature of logic that had defeated Russell himself and to become the standard-bearer in the fight to establish 'scientific method in philosophy'. When the next big step was finally taken, it took the form of saying that the problems about the nature of logic could only be solved when one understood the confusions that gave rise to them, and one of those confusions was precisely the conviction that there could possibly be such a thing as scientific method in philosophy.

6

THE DISINTEGRATION OF LOGICAL FORM

Every proposition has a content and a form. We get the picture of the pure form if we abstract from the meaning of the single words, or symbols (so far as they have independent meanings). That is to say, if we substitute variables for the constants of the proposition. The rules of syntax which applied to the constants must apply to the variables also. By syntax in this general sense of the word I mean the rules which tell us in which connections only a word gives sense, thus excluding nonsensical structures. The syntax of ordinary language, as is well known, is not quite adequate for this purpose. It does not in all cases prevent the construction of nonsensical pseudo-propositions (constructions such as 'red is higher than green' or 'the Real, though it is an *in itself*, must also be able to become a *for myself*', etc.).

If we try to analyse any given propositions we shall find in general that they are logical sums, products or other truth-functions of simpler propositions. But our analysis, if carried far enough, must come to the point where it reaches propositional forms which are not themselves composed of simpler propositional forms. We must eventually reach the ultimate connection of the terms, the immediate connection which cannot be broken without destroying the propositional form as such. The propositions which represent this ultimate connection of terms I call, after B. Russell, atomic propositions. They, then, are the kernels of every proposition, *they* contain the material, and all the rest is only a development of this material. It is to them we have to look for the subject matter of propositions. It is the task of the theory of knowledge to find them and to understand their construction out of the words or symbols. This task is very difficult, and Philosophy has hardly yet begun to tackle it at some points. What method have we for tackling it? The idea is to express in an appropriate symbolism what in ordinary language leads to endless misunderstandings. That is to say, where ordinary language disguises logical structure, where it allows the formation of pseudo-propositions, where it uses one term in an infinity of different meanings, we must replace it by a symbolism which gives a clear picture of the logical structure, excludes pseudo-propositions, and uses its terms unambiguously . . .

The mutual exclusion of unanalysable statements of degree contradicts an opinion which was published by me several years ago and which necessitated that atomic propositions could not exclude one another. I here deliberately say 'exclude' and not 'contradict', for there is a difference between these two notions, and atomic propositions, although they cannot contradict, may exclude one another. There are functions which can give a true proposition only for one value of their argument because – if I may so express myself – there is only room in them for one.

Take, for instance, a proposition which asserts the existence of a colour R at a certain time T in a certain place P
of our visual field. I will write this proposition 'R P T', and
abstract for the moment from any consideration of how
such a statement is to be further analysed. 'B P T', then,
says that the colour B is in the place P at the time T,
and it will be clear to most of us here, and to all of us in
ordinary life, that 'R P T & B P T' is some sort of contradiction (and not merely a false proposition). Now if
statements of degree were analysable – as I used to think –
we could explain this contradiction by saying that the
colour R contains all degrees of R and none of B and that
the colour B contains all degrees of B and none of R. But
from the above it follows that no analysis can eliminate
statements of degree. How, then, does the mutual exclusion of R P T and B P T operate? I believe it consists in the
fact that R P T as well as B P T are in a certain sense
complete. That which corresponds in reality to the function
'( ) P T' leaves room only for one entity – in the same
sense, in fact, in which we say that there is room for one
person only in a chair. Our symbolism, which allows us to
form the sign of the logical product of 'R P T' and 'B P T'
gives here no correct picture of reality.

'Some Remarks on Logical Form', 1929

In accordance with his view that *Tractatus Logico-Philosophicus*
solved all the problems of philosophy, Wittgenstein gave up
philosophy after the book was finished. He trained to be a
schoolteacher instead, and, for six, largely unhappy, years,
1920–26, he taught at various elementary schools in the coun-
tryside south of Vienna. He was teaching in the village of
Puchberg when the *Tractatus* was published, and, while he

continued to live in rural isolation, his book became the centre of great interest among academics in Cambridge and in Vienna. One of the most perceptive readers of the book was Frank Ramsey, who, though still an undergraduate, was widely regarded at Cambridge as a mathematician and a philosopher of great promise. Ramsey had helped with the English edition of the book and wrote a long and insightful review of it for *Mind*. In the summer of 1923, Wittgenstein heard from Ogden that Ramsey planned to visit Vienna and at once wrote to him to invite him to Puchberg. He arrived on 17 September and stayed for about two weeks, during which time, Wittgenstein – thinking, perhaps, that Ramsey might potentially be the one comprehending reader he was looking for – devoted five hours a day to going through the book line by line with him. The result was that Ramsey returned to Cambridge with the conviction that Wittgenstein should abandon his self-imposed exile from academic life, and Wittgenstein began to think, under Ramsey's astute questioning, that the *Tractatus* was not, after all, the last word on its subject.

Wittgenstein left teaching in the spring of 1926 and returned to Vienna, working first as a gardener, and then as an architect, designing a striking house for his sister, notable for its austere, unadorned beauty. In the meantime, Wittgenstein began a gradual return to philosophy. In 1927, he started attending regular meetings of a group of philosophers based at the University of Vienna, led by Moritz Schlick. This group was to become famous as the 'Vienna Circle', and the 'logical positivism' they espoused was to become widely influential in analytic philosophy. Throughout 1928, Wittgenstein's interest in philosophy was increasingly revived and he became convinced that he should, after all, return to the subject in order to rethink some aspects of the *Tractatus*. In the New Year of 1929, he returned to Cambridge, officially as an 'Advanced Student' reading for a Ph.D. with Ramsey, seventeen years his junior and now a Fellow of King's, as his supervisor.

Within six months Wittgenstein had written the paper that would become his third and last publication. The paper is called 'Some Remarks on Logical Form' and was written to be presented at the Annual Joint Session of the Aristotelian Society and the Mind Association, the most important and prestigious annual conference of academic philosophers in Britain. Although the paper was published in the conference proceedings, Wittgenstein never actually gave it. So quickly was his thought developing at this time that, as soon as he delivered it, he disowned it as worthless, and at the meeting read something quite different, something on the concept of infinity, no trace of which has survived.

'Some Remarks on Logical Form' is nevertheless interesting as a record of how and why the logical edifice of the *Tractatus* came tumbling down and with it the whole notion of 'logical form' that played such a central role in Wittgenstein's early thought.

The initial damage was done by Frank Ramsey, who, in his review of the *Tractatus* pointed out a problem for Wittgenstein's view of logical necessity. 'Just as the only necessity that exists is *logical* necessity,' Wittgenstein says in proposition 6.375, 'so too the only impossibility that exists is *logical* impossibility.' In the following proposition, 6.3751, he goes on to say: 'For example, the simultaneous presence of two colours at the same place in the visual field is impossible, in fact logically impossible, since it is ruled out by the logical structure of colour.' He also says a little later in the same proposition: 'It is clear that the logical product of two atomic propositions can neither be a tautology nor a contradiction.

The statement that a point in the visual field has two different colours at the same time is a contradiction.' It follows that a proposition ascribing a certain colour to a point in the visual field ('This is red', 'This is blue', etc.) cannot be an *atomic* proposition, i.e., such a proposition must be capable of further analysis. In the *Tractatus*, Wittgenstein appeals, rather unconvincingly, to a physical analysis of colour in terms of the velocities of particles (one must assume that he did not know, at this point, the theory, now universally accepted, that light always has the same velocity and that different colours are to be analysed in terms of wave-frequencies rather than particle velocities). The impossibility of something's being both red and blue at the same time thus appears as the statement that a particle cannot have two velocities at the same time. However, as Ramsey pointed out, this purported physical analysis – even if it had any scientific basis (which it does not) – does not get rid of the problem: '. . . even supposing that the physicist thus provides an analysis of what we mean by "red", Mr Wittgenstein is only reducing the difficulty to that of the *necessary* properties of space, time and matter or the ether. He explicitly makes it depend upon the *impossibility* of a particle being in two places at the same time.' It is hard to see, says Ramsey, how *this* impossibility can be a matter of logic rather than physics, which it would have to be if Wittgenstein is to hold on to his view that the only necessity is logical necessity. If Wittgenstein is not to give up this claim, he has to show how the properties of space, time and matter can appear as *logical* necessities.

In 'Some Remarks on Logical Form' Wittgenstein attempts to solve this problem by making a fairly drastic change to his notion of an atomic proposition, a change that was to bring the entire theory of the *Tractatus* crashing to the ground. The change sounds technical and minor. It consisted in surrendering the view that atomic propositions are logically independent of one another. *Some* atomic propositions, Wittgenstein now holds, are mutually exclusive. If a point in the visual field is red, it cannot also be blue, or green, or yellow, etc. Thus, 'This is red and this is blue' is a contradiction, *even though* it is a conjunction of atomic propositions. This means that Wittgenstein has to give up the claim about facts in proposition 1.21: 'Each item can be the case or not the case while everything else remains the same.' He also has to give up what he says about logic, for now an 'adequate symbolism' is *not* sufficient to tell us whether a particular conjunction of propositions is or is not a contradiction. Not all contradictions are like 'It is raining and it is not raining'. I.e., not all of them can be symbolized as 'p and not-p'. Some of them are symbolized as 'p and q', which is not very helpful, because most conjunctions symbolized as 'p and q' are *not* contradictions.

With this apparently minor and technical concession, then, the whole theory falls apart, and Wittgenstein is left, not with the problem of repairing holes in the theory of the *Tractatus* but with that of fundamentally rethinking his entire approach to logic and language. This is what he did in the years following his return to Cambridge in 1929, and, by the mid-1930s, he had developed a radically different way of dealing with philosophical problems, one that has become known as 'Wittgenstein's later philosophy'.

THE NEW PHILOSOPHY: GIVING UP THE CRYSTALLINE PURITY OF LOGIC

107. The more narrowly we examine actual language, the sharper becomes the conflict between it and our requirement. (For the crystalline purity of logic was, of course, not a *result of investigation*: it was a requirement.) The conflict becomes intolerable; the requirement is now in danger of becoming empty. —We have got on to slippery ice where there is no friction and so in a certain sense the conditions are ideal, but also, just because of that, we are unable to walk. We want to walk; so we need *friction*. Back to the rough ground!

108. We see that what we call 'sentence' and 'language' has not the formal unity that I imagined, but is the family of structures more or less related to one another. —But what becomes of logic now? Its rigour seems to be giving way here. —But in that case doesn't logic altogether disappear? —For how can it lose its rigour? Of course not by our bargaining any of its rigour out of it. —The *preconceived idea* of crystalline purity can only be removed by turning our whole examination round . . .

109. It was true to say that our considerations could not be scientific ones. It was not of any possible interest to us to

find out empirically 'that, contrary to our preconceived ideas, it is possible to think such-and-such' – whatever that may mean. (The conception of thought as a gaseous medium.) And we may not advance any kind of theory. There must not be anything hypothetical in our considerations. We must do away with all *explanation*, and description alone must take its place. And this description gets its light, that is to say its purpose, from the philosophical problems. These are, of course, not empirical problems; they are solved, rather, by looking into the workings of our language, and that in such a way as to make us recognize those workings: *in despite of* an urge to misunderstand them. The problems are solved, not by giving new information, but by arranging what we have always known. Philosophy is a battle against the bewitchment of our intelligence by means of language.

Philosophical Investigations, 1953

In the summer of 1929, six months after he returned to Cambridge as an 'Advanced Student', Wittgenstein was awarded a Ph.D. for the *Tractatus*, a work that had been in print for seven years and was already regarded by many as a philosophical classic. In 1930, he began to give lectures, which quickly attracted the attention of the entire philosophical community after it became known that, in them, Wittgenstein was developing an entirely new way of approaching philosophical problems.

From the early 1930s until his death in 1951, Wittgenstein tried again and again to construct a book that would present his new philosophical outlook to the world. He died without completing the job to his satisfaction, and it was left to his literary executors to publish *Philosophical Investigations* in the incomplete state in which Wittgenstein left it. Since then, many of the manuscripts and typescripts that constitute Wittgenstein's *Nachlass* have been published as 'works' by Wittgenstein – *Philosophical Remarks*, *Philosophical Grammar*, *The Blue and Brown Books*, *Remarks on the Philosophy of Mathematics*, *Remarks on the Philosophy of Psychology*, *On Certainty*, *On Colour*, etc. Though all of these contain important philosophical writings, it should be borne in mind that none of them, not even *Philosophical Investigations*, can be regarded as a book by Wittgenstein.

The difficulties Wittgenstein had in finishing a book that presented his later philosophy are connected with the nature of that philosophy. In *Tractatus Logico-Philosophicus*, Wittgenstein had said that philosophy was an activity not a doctrine and that there could be no such things as philosophical propositions. Nevertheless, despite this, he produced a book consisting for the most part in sentences that certainly *look* as if they are intended to be philosophical propositions, espousing what looks like a doctrine, a theory about logical form. In his later work, Wittgenstein was much more rigorous in eschewing theory and pursuing philosophy as an activity. Precisely because of that, however, it was insuperably difficult for him to construct a *book* that presented his new method.

At several times Wittgenstein thought he had got close to finishing *Philosophical Investigations*. He wanted to publish it side by side with *Tractatus Logico-Philosophicus*, because so many of the remarks he wanted to include in this new book alluded to views he had published in the *Tractatus*. But, more than that, he felt that his new work could be understood *only* with reference to his early work.

This is partly because of the great differences between his early and later work, but also because of the equally important continuities between the two. Wittgenstein never repudiated the remarks about philosophy quoted earlier from the *Tractatus*. Rather, he began to understand better what was required in order to do justice to the insights that those remarks expressed; for example, that there can be no such thing as a philosophical proposition, and that philosophy was *entirely different* to science.

He began to think that, in not properly understanding these insights when he wrote *Tractatus*, he had fallen into precisely the kind of errors that characterize philosophy. Chief among these was his presupposition that there was a single 'logical form' shared by thought, language and the world, which a philosopher might uncover and reveal. During his first six months back in Cambridge in 1929, as he wrestled with the difficulties about logical form that Ramsey had raised, he fairly quickly came to the conclusion that the very notion of logical form had to be abandoned. In this, he was helped by conversations with Ramsey and, still more, by conversations with the Italian economist Piero Sraffa. In the preface to *Philosophical Investigations* that he wrote in 1945, Wittgenstein says that he is indebted to Sraffa for 'the most consequential ideas of this book'. A clue as to what he meant by this very large statement is contained in a story that Wittgenstein told his friend Norman Malcolm. According to the story, Wittgenstein, soon after his return to Cambridge, was explaining his ideas to Sraffa and was insisting – as he had insisted in *Tractatus* – that a proposition and that which it describes must have the same 'logical form'. To this, Sraffa made a Neapolitan gesture of brushing his chin with his fingertips, asking: 'What is the logical form of *that*?'

The story provides a good example of the kind of thing Wittgenstein means when he says in the passage quoted above that certain preconceived ideas in philosophy can only be got rid of by 'turning our whole examination round'. We need to look at the problems afresh, as it were from a different angle. In fact, this is *all* that we need in philosophy; we do not need a new discovery, we do not need a new explanation and we do not need a new theory; what we need is a new perspective, a new metaphor, a new picture. Wittgenstein's style in *Tractatus Logico-Philosophicus* reflected what he here describes (and ridicules) as the requirement for the crystalline purity of logic. His new style is very different. Gone is the icy rigour of numbered propositions that give the appearance of wanting to belong to a mathematical demonstration, and in its place is a more colloquial style, full of inventive similes and metaphors. The conviction that philosophy ought to be written only as a poetic composition is still at work, only now the emphasis is not on showing the reader things that cannot be said, but on getting the reader to *see* things afresh.

> 122. A main source of our failure to understand is that we do not *command a clear view* of the use of our words. — Our grammar is lacking in this sort of perspicuity. A perspicuous representation produces just that understanding which consists in 'seeing connections'. Hence the importance of finding and inventing *intermediate cases*.
>
> The concept of a perspicuous representation is of fundamental significance for us. It earmarks the form of account we give, the way we look at things. (Is this a '*Weltanschauung*'?)

Whereas, previously, Wittgenstein had offered the reader a *theory*, albeit one of a very peculiar sort – one that destroyed itself from within, that said of itself that it was nonsense – now he eschews theory and explanation altogether, putting in their place description and what he calls *Übersicht*, usually translated, as above, as 'perspicuous representation'.

As he says here, this notion of an *Übersicht* was of fundamental significance for his later philosophy. An *Übersicht* produces the 'understanding which consists in "seeing connections"', which is, Wittgenstein believes, the kind of understanding after which philosophers ought to seek. The contrast here is with the kind of understanding that is produced by a theory or an explanation. The contrast between the two has something in common with his earlier contrast between what can be said and what can only be shown, only it does not appeal to anything mystical. What it appeals to is something that is at once more common and, in our increasingly scientistic society, less well understood, namely the kind of understanding we have of, and can be given to us by, a piece of music, a poem or a work of art.

Wittgenstein's notion of an *Übersicht* and of what it could achieve was heavily influenced by the work of one of his literary heroes, Johann Wolfgang von Goethe, who, in addition to the poetry and fiction that established him as one of the greatest ever German writers, wrote a number of works outlining his notion of a *morphological* study of nature, which he considered to be a rival to the mathematical methods favoured by conventional physics, chemistry and biology. These morphological studies – the *Metamorphosis of Plants* and the *Metamorphosis of Animals* – had as their motivation Goethe's disgust with the mechanism of Newtonian science. He wanted to replace what he considered to be a dead, mechanical study with a discipline that sought to 'recognize living forms *as such*, to see in context their visible and tangible parts, to perceive them as *manifestations* of something within'. What Goethe did was to study plants and animals, not by looking for mathematical regularities and causal laws, but by *seeing* the connections between one plant and another, one animal and another. As the cultural historian Oswald Spengler – who took Goethe's notion of morphology and applied it to the study of human culture and civilization and who was also cited by Wittgenstein as an influence – put it in *The Decline of the West*: 'The means whereby to identify dead forms is Mathematical Law. The means whereby to identify living forms is Analogy.'

Wittgenstein took this notion from Goethe and Spengler and applied it to language, seeing language now not as a manifestation of the 'crystalline purity of logic' but as a rich variety of *living* forms that resisted the attempts by logicians to impose upon it a unitary logical form. 'What I give,' Wittgenstein once said in a lecture, 'is the morphology of the use of an expression.' Elsewhere, he wrote: 'Our thought here marches with certain views of Goethe's which he expressed in the *Metamorphosis of Plants* . . . We are collating one form of language with its environment, or transforming it in imagination so as to gain a view of the whole space in which the structure of our language has its being.'

Increasingly, Wittgenstein thought of himself as pursuing a campaign against the dominant cultural trends in our society. In 1938, he told his students: 'I am in a sense making propaganda for one style of thinking as opposed to another. I am honestly disgusted with the other. Also I'm trying to state what I think. Nevertheless I'm saying: "For God's sake don't do this."'

Don't do what? The answer seems to be: don't worship science. Immediately before the above remark, Wittgenstein said in his lecture: 'Jeans has written a book called *The Mysterious Universe* and I loathe it and call it misleading. Take the title. This alone I would call misleading . . . I might say the title *The Mysterious Universe* includes a kind of idol worship, the idol being Science and the Scientist.'

The search for explanations and theories in philosophy, Wittgenstein believed, was linked with this worship of science. Intoxicated by the success of science, philosophers had forgotten that there was another kind of understanding. 'People nowadays think that scientists exist to instruct them,' he once wrote in a notebook, 'poets, musicians, etc. to give them pleasure. The idea *that these have something to teach them –* that does not occur to them.'

Russell, of course, was horrified by this attitude. 'The later Wittgenstein,' he wrote, 'seems to have grown tired of serious thinking and to have invented a doctrine which would make such an activity unnecessary.' If one thinks that 'serious thinking' and 'science' are the same thing, then this remark is precisely right. Another way of looking at it, though, is to think that philosophers can only possibly think seriously when they free themselves from any lingering belief that their subject is, or could possibly be, a kind of science.

8

LANGUAGE GAMES

I shall in the future again and again draw your attention to what I shall call language games. These are ways of using signs simpler than those in which we use the signs of our highly complicated everyday language. Language games are the forms of language with which a child begins to make use of words. The study of language games is the study of primitive forms of language or primitive languages. If we want to study the problems of truth and falsehood, of the agreement and disagreement of propositions with reality, of the nature of assertion, assumption, and question, we shall with great advantage look at primitive forms of language in which these forms of thinking appear without the confusing background of highly complicated processes of thought. When we look at such simple forms of language the mental mist which seems to enshroud our ordinary use of language disappears. We see activities, reactions, which are clear-cut and transparent. On the other hand we recognize in these simple processes forms of language not separated by a break from our more complicated ones. We see that we can build up the complicated forms from the primitive ones by gradually adding new forms.

Now what makes it difficult for us to take this line of investigation is our craving for generality.

This craving for generality is the resultant of a number of tendencies connected with particular philosophical confusions. There is –

(a) The tendency to look for something in common to all the entities which we commonly subsume under a general term. —We are inclined to think that there must be something in common to all games, say, and that this common property is the justification for applying the general term 'game' to the various games; whereas games form a *family*, the members of which have family likenesses. Some of them have the same nose, others the same eyebrows and others again the same way of walking; and these likenesses overlap.

(b) There is a tendency rooted in our usual forms of expression to think that the man who has learned to understand a general term, say, the term 'leaf', has thereby come to possess a kind of general picture of a leaf, as opposed to pictures of particular leaves. He was shown different leaves when he learned the meaning of the word 'leaf'; and showing him the particular leaves was only a means to the end of producing 'in him' an idea which we imagine to be some kind of general image. We say that he sees what is common to all these leaves; and this is true if we mean that he can on being asked tell us certain features or properties which they have in common. But we are inclined to think that the general idea of a leaf is something like a visual image, but one which contains what is common to all leaves. (Galtonian composite photograph.) This again is connected with the idea that the meaning of a word is an image, or a thing correlated to the word. (This roughly means, we are looking at words as though they all were proper names, and we then confuse the bearer of a name with the meaning of the name.)

(c) Again the idea we have of what happens when we get hold of the general idea 'leaf', 'plant', etc., etc., is connected with the confusion between a mental state, meaning a state of a hypothetical mental mechanism, and a mental state meaning a state of consciousness (toothache, etc.).

(d) Our craving for generality has another main source: our preoccupation with the method of science. I mean the method of reducing the explanation of natural phenomena to the smallest possible number of primitive natural laws; and, in mathematics, of unifying the treatment of different topics by using a generalization. Philosophers constantly see the method of science before their eyes, and are irresistibly tempted to ask and answer questions in the way science does. This tendency is the real source of metaphysics, and leads the philosopher into complete darkness.

The Blue Book, pp. 17–18

In the academic year of 1933–34, Wittgenstein's lectures were attracting far more students (between thirty and forty) than he felt comfortable lecturing to, and so he announced that he would dictate his lectures to a small group of students who would then copy them and distribute them to the others. The set of notes he dictated was bound in blue covers and became known as 'The Blue Book'. As it was the first publication in any form of Wittgenstein's new method of philosophy, it created great interest. Further copies were made and, within a few years, it was being distributed in Oxford, London and even in colleges in the United States. *The Blue Book* was thus responsible for introducing into philosophic discourse the notion that, for many, is the key to Wittgenstein's later philosophy: the 'language game'.

There are many prevalent misconceptions of this notion, the most widespread of which is to take it to be a *theoretical* notion, a key component of a general theory of language. It should be clear from the previous chapter (and from almost everything Wittgenstein wrote after 1930) that the construction of a general theory of language was the very last thing he wanted to achieve. Nevertheless, it is not uncommon to read commentators talk about Wittgenstein's 'theory of language games'. Sometimes it is imagined that Wittgenstein thought of language games as entirely separate 'islands of discourse' – there would be a language game of science, a language game of religion, etc. – each isolated from the others. Even well-informed commentators sometimes talk as if Wittgenstein introduced the notion of a language game in order to say what the constituent parts of a language were.

It seems to me that the best way of understanding the use Wittgenstein makes of language games is to see their role in the construction of an *Übersicht*, and thereby their role in producing 'the kind of understanding that consists in seeing connections'.

In *Tractatus Logico-Philosophicus*, Wittgenstein had said that philosophical problems arise because the logic of our language is misunderstood. His attempted solution was to produce a correct account of the logic of our language. But when this collapsed, he began to see things completely differently, to question whether there *is* something that could be called *the* logic of our language. Indeed, he now takes his own earlier work as a perfect example of how philosophers are misled. For notice that what he says above about 'the craving for generality' applies to the author of *Tractatus Logico-Philosophicus* as much as to any other philosopher. When, in the *Tractatus*, Wittgenstein had attempted to analyse 'the general form of the proposition', he had fallen victim to the 'tendency to look for something in common to all the entities which we commonly subsume under a general term', thinking that there must be a single form that was common to *all* propositions.

His proposed remedy to these kinds of confusions is to keep reminding the philosopher of trivialities, such as: not all meaningful uses of language are meaningful in the *same* way. For example, names acquire their meaning through being correlated with a person or object, but (a) not all words are names and (b) the thing or person that is the *bearer* of the name is not itself or herself the *meaning* of the name. When, for example, Bertrand Russell died, the meaning of his name did not die. To say this kind of thing, Wittgenstein believes (surely rightly), is not to advance a *theory*; it is just to point out something that is obviously true but which the philosopher, in the grip, as he or she is, of a particular picture or presupposition, is often liable to forget. In the *Tractatus*, for example, Wittgenstein wrote: 'A name means an object. The object is its meaning', and he also put forward the idea that an atomic proposition contained nothing *but* names, that *all* the words of which it is composed are the representatives of objects. Now, of course, Wittgenstein knew that, in the ordinary sense, not all words *were* names, but, in pursuing his definitive and unassailably true solution to the problems of philosophy, he chose to ignore this obvious truth.

The way that Wittgenstein now proposes to clear up philosophical confusions bears some similarities to Freudian psychoanalysis ('The philosopher's treatment of a problem is like a doctor's treatment of an illness'). There are some arguments in Wittgenstein's later work, but not enough for the taste of most professional philosophers. In most cases, Wittgenstein does not offer an *argument*, but rather a kind of *therapy*. In his conversations and lectures, Wittgenstein drew attention to the analogy between his philosophical method and Freud's psychological methods, even to the extent of describing himself as a 'disciple of Freud'. However, he had no sympathy whatever for Freud's own conception of his achievement, according to which he had created a new *science* of psychology. For Wittgenstein, it was absolutely vital to realize that Freud had *not* given us a set of scientific explanations for, e.g., dreams and neuroses. His achievement was much greater than *that*, for what Freud had given us, according to Wittgenstein, was a new *mythology*, a new way of looking at ourselves and the people around us, a way that allowed us to see connections between things that we had not seen before.

And *this* is what Wittgenstein hoped to achieve with the method of inventing language games. He hoped that they might play a useful role in the 'therapy' required to get a philosopher to acknowledge that his or her philosophical theory is just a confusion built upon a misconception. A language game is a (usually fictitious) primitive form of language in which one particular aspect of our ordinary language – say, the role of names – is highlighted by being separated from the complicated contexts in which it is usually embedded. The idea is that we will be able to 'see the connection' between this simplified case and language as it is used in real life.

Take, for example, the language game that appears in the very first paragraph of *Philosophical Investigations*:

Now think of the following use of language: I send someone shopping. I give him a slip marked 'five red apples'. He takes the slip to the shopkeeper, who opens the drawer marked 'apples'; then he looks up the word 'red' in a table and finds a colour sample opposite it; then he says the series of cardinal numbers – I assume that he knows them by heart – up to the word 'five' and for each number he takes an apple of the same colour as the sample out of the drawer. —It is in this and similar ways that one operates with words.

The most natural reaction to this last sentence is to say: 'No, it isn't! Whoever heard of a shopkeeper who keeps his apples in a drawer? And when have you ever seen somebody appeal to a colour chart in order to decide what is and what is not *red*? Admittedly, some people *do* say out loud "one, two, three, four, five" when counting five things, but the more normal case is just to take five things, put them in a bag and hand them to the customer, without saying anything. What Wittgenstein has described here is definitely *not* the way we operate with words!'

Clearly, Wittgenstein does not intend this invented language game to mirror reality in all its complexity, but neither would he claim to have presented any aspect of language 'in its essence' (in the way, for example, that he claimed in *Tractatus Logico-Philosophicus* to have presented the 'essence' of the proposition). No, this fictitious, in some ways utterly unrealistic, scenario is designed to present *some* aspects of our language in a way that is more primitive than that in which they appear in our everyday lives. And the point of that is to enable us to see more clearly than we would otherwise do some features of our language that we might otherwise overlook. For, though the scene played out here would never be mistaken for a scene that might actually happen in real life when a man goes to a shop to buy five red apples, nevertheless it is quite possible to 'see the connections' between the words 'five red apples' as they are used here and as they are used in ordinary life.

Wittgenstein's point in the above example is to draw attention to what philosophers customarily pass over: namely, the *differences* in the ways we use words. Anyone who could, as Wittgenstein did in *Tractatus*, regard all names as operating in fundamentally the same way, has clearly not considered the differences between: a) the names of numbers, b) the names of colours and c) the names of objects. Every word in the phrase 'five red apples' is a name, but how differently we use each kind of name is brought out in the 'primitive' way in which the characters in Wittgenstein's imagined language game go about their business.

The shopkeeper keeps his apples in a drawer marked 'apples'. This seems absurd, but it is, after all, *possible*. But, could he keep numbers in a drawer marked 'numbers'? Or colours in a drawer marked 'colours'? Then he looks up the word 'red' in a table. If this seems ridiculous, consider what Wittgenstein writes in *The Blue Book*:

> There is one way of avoiding at least partly the occult appearance of the processes of thinking, and it is to replace in these processes any working of the imagination by acts of looking at real objects. Thus it may seem essential that, at least in certain cases, when I hear the word 'red' with understanding, a red image should be before my mind's eye. But why should I not substitute seeing a red bit of paper for imagining a red patch? The visual image will only be more vivid. Imagine a man always carrying a sheet of paper in his

pocket in which the names of colours are co-ordinated with coloured patches.

In other words, when the shopkeeper looks up the word 'red' in a table, he is doing something strictly analogous to what many philosophers and psychologists have claimed we all do in our minds. Our understanding of the word 'red', it is often claimed, requires us to have a kind of colour chart in our imagination, which we use to compare what we see to what we 'associate' with the word. Well, says Wittgenstein, if that *is* how we use the word, then surely a colour chart in our hand is as good as, if not better than, one in our minds.

As for the shopkeeper counting out the numbers, well the point here is that the word 'five' requires, for it to have the meaning it *does* have, the entire system of cardinal numbers. The word is not used, and cannot be used, as a label for something in a drawer or for something on a chart; for it to have the meaning it has, the activity of counting has to be pre-supposed. A community in which nobody could count is a community in which the word 'five' would have no use, which is to say, no meaning.

Wittgenstein introduces the language game discussed above immediately after quoting a passage from St Augustine's *Confessions* in which Augustine describes how he learned to speak his mother tongue. In English (Wittgenstein quotes it first in Latin), the passage is as follows:

When they (my elders) named some object, and accordingly moved towards something, I saw this and I grasped that the thing was called by the sound they uttered when they meant to point it out. Their intention was shown by their bodily movements, as it were the natural language of all peoples: the expression of the face, the play of the eyes, the movement of other parts of the body, and the tone of voice which expresses our state of mind in seeking, having, rejecting, or avoiding something. Thus, as I heard words repeatedly used in their proper places in various sentences, I gradually learned to understand what objects they signified; and after I had trained my mouth to form these signs, I used them to express my own desires.

It is sometimes said that Wittgenstein's point in quoting this passage at the beginning of the *Investigations* is to articulate the theory of language that forms the target of his work, a theory he will show to be false. This, I think, is quite wrong. *Confessions* is not a theoretical work of philosophy, it is an autobiography; and Augustine's purpose in the passage quoted above is not to theorize about language, it is to describe how he learned to speak.

However, precisely *because* of this, the passage forms the ideal starting point for *Philosophical Investigations*. For the aim of Wittgenstein's later work is not to argue *against* the views and theories of other philosophers, to show that these views and theories are false; it is, rather, to attack philosophical confusions at their *source*. At the time of writing *Tractatus Logico-Philosophicus*, Wittgenstein had believed that to become involved in a philosophical debate (as Russell had become involved in the debate with Bradley about whether or not relations exist) is already to have lost. *All* philosophical theories are nonsense; the way to solve philosophical problems was to clear the confusions about logic and language that had given rise to them. Analogously, in his later work, Wittgenstein treats *all* philosophical doctrines as confusions, though now he thinks the confusion has arisen because, as he puts it, 'a picture held us captive'. His task is to free us from that picture. Because the picture that held us captive and that gave rise to the philosophical problem is *assumed* in everything we say, it cannot usually be dislodged by argument. It is, as it were, too deep for that. What is required to free us from the picture that holds us captive is an enriched *imagination*, and this cannot be given to us through argument, it must be acquired through, as it were, therapy. Wittgenstein's later work, then, is aimed at the pre-philosophical, rather than the philosophical, level. It addresses, not our argumentative faculties, but our imagination.

Though this point is often overlooked by commentators, Wittgenstein could hardly have done more to make it clear. It is spelled out in the very first sentences of the book. Immediately after quoting St Augustine, Wittgenstein writes:

> These words, it seems to me, give us a particular *picture* of the essence of human language. It is this: the individual words in language name objects – sentences are combinations of such names. —In this *picture* of language we find the roots of the following *idea*: Every word has a meaning. The meaning is correlated with the word. It is the object for which the word stands. [my italics]

Why does Wittgenstein distinguish here between the picture and the idea? Because, I think, he wants to get at the *root* of the difficulty. To argue against the idea, while leaving the picture in place, would be a waste of time. What is required is to replace one picture with another.

In the second paragraph of *Philosophical Investigations*, Wittgenstein offers another language game, one, he says, that imagines 'a language for which the description given by

Augustine is right'. I.e., it is a language that consists entirely of nouns:

> The language is meant to serve for communication between a builder A and an assistant B. A is building with building-stones: there are blocks, pillars, slabs and beams. B has to pass the stones, and that in the order in which A needs them. For this purpose they use a language consisting of the words 'block', 'pillar', 'slab', 'beam'. A calls them out; – B brings the stone which he has learned to bring at such-and-such a call. —Conceive this as a complete primitive language.

A few paragraphs later, Wittgenstein asks us to imagine an expansion to this language:

> Besides the four words 'block', 'pillar', etc., let it contain a series of words used as the shopkeeper in (1) used the numerals (it can be the series of letters of the alphabet); further, let there be two words, which may as well be 'there' and 'this' (because this roughly indicates their purpose), that are used in connection with a pointing gesture; and finally a number of colour samples. A gives an order like: 'd-slab – there'. At the same time he shews the assistant a colour sample, and when he says 'there' he points to a place on the building site. From the stock of slabs B takes one for each letter of the alphabet up to 'd', of the same colour as the sample, and brings them to the place indicated by A. —On other occasions A gives the order 'this–there'. At 'this' he points to a building stone. And so on.

'Now,' Wittgenstein asks, 'what do the words of this language *signify*?' He answers: 'What is supposed to shew what they signify, if not the kind of use they have? And we have already described that.' If we were not happy with this answer, if we insisted that there must be more to the signification of the words than the ways in which they are used, then we *could* say, for example, that, just as the word 'slab' signified a kind of stone, so 'b' signified a particular number: 'But assimilating the descriptions of the uses of words in this way cannot make the uses themselves any more like one another. For, as we see, they are absolutely unlike.'

In *Tractatus Logico-Philosophicus*, Wittgenstein had investigated *one* form of language: the assertoric sentence, or 'proposition'. His defence of this was to say that other forms of language, questions and commands, can be regarded as modified assertions, so that a common core to all three can be identified (e.g., from 'The door is shut', we can derive 'Is the door shut?' and 'Shut the door!'). Thus, by investigating the logical form of propositions, we can legitimately claim to be investigating the structure of our whole language. Using the notion of a language game, Wittgenstein now exposes this view to a merciless attack:

> But how many kinds of sentence are there? Say assertion, question, and command? —There are *countless* kinds: countless different kinds of use of what we call 'symbols', 'words', 'sentences'. And this multiplicity is not something fixed, given once for all; but new types of language, new language games, as we may say, come into existence, and others become obsolete and get forgotten. (We can get a *rough picture* of this from the changes in mathematics.)
>
> Here the term 'language *game*' is meant to bring into

prominence the fact that the *speaking* of language is part of an activity, or of a form of life.

Review the multiplicity of language games in the following examples, and in others:

Giving orders, and obeying them—
Describing the appearance of an object, or giving its measurements—
Constructing an object from a description (a drawing)—
Reporting an event—
Speculating about an event—
Forming and testing a hypothesis—
Presenting the results of an experiment in tables and diagrams—
Making up a story; and reading it—
Play-acting—
Singing catches—
Guessing riddles—
Making a joke; telling it—
Solving a problem in practical arithmetic—
Translating from one language into another—
Asking, thanking, cursing, greeting, praying.

—It is interesting to compare the multiplicity of the tools in language and of the ways they are used, the multiplicity of kinds of word and sentence, with what logicians have said about the structure of language. (Including the author of the *Tractatus Logico-Philosophicus.*)

9

CAN THERE BE A PRIVATE LANGUAGE?

243. A human being can encourage himself, give himself orders, obey, blame and punish himself; he can ask himself a question and answer it. We could even imagine human beings who spoke only in monologue; who accompanied their activities by talking to themselves. —An explorer who watched them and listened to their talk might succeed in translating their language into ours. (This would enable him to predict these people's actions correctly, for he also hears them making resolutions and decisions.)

But could we also imagine a language in which a person could write down or give vocal expression to his inner experiences – his feelings, moods, and the rest – for his private use? —Well, can't we do so in our ordinary language? —But that is not what I mean. The individual words of this language are to refer to what can only be known to the person speaking; to his immediate private sensations. So another person cannot understand the language.

244. How do words *refer* to sensations? —There doesn't seem to be any problem here; don't we talk about sensations every day, and give them names? But how is the

connection between the name and the things named set up? This question is the same as: how does a human being learn the meaning of the names of sensations? – of the word 'pain' for example. Here is one possibility: words are connected with the primitive, the natural, expressions of the sensation and used in their place. A child has hurt himself and he cries; and then adults talk to him and teach him exclamations and, later, sentences. They teach the child new pain-behaviour.

'So you are saying that the word "pain" really means crying?' —On the contrary: the verbal expression of pain replaces crying and does not describe it.

245. For how can I go so far as to try to use language to get between pain and its expression?

246. In what sense are my sensations *private*? —Well, only I can know whether I am really in pain; another person can only surmise it. —In one way this is wrong, and in another nonsense. If we are using the word 'to know' as it is normally used (and how else are we to use it?), then other people very often know when I am in pain. —Yes, but all the same not with the certainty with which I know it myself! —It can't be said of me at all (except perhaps as a joke) that I *know* I am in pain. What is it supposed to mean – except perhaps that I *am* in pain?

Other people cannot be said to learn of my sensations *only* from my behaviour – for *I* cannot be said to learn of them. I *have* them.

The truth is: it makes sense to say about other people that they doubt whether I am in pain; but not to say it about myself.

247. 'Only you can know if you had that intention.' One might tell someone this when one was explaining the

meaning of the word 'intention' to him. For then it means: *that* is how we use it.

(And here 'know' means that the expression of uncertainty is senseless.)

248. The proposition 'Sensations are private' is comparable to: 'One plays patience by oneself.'

. . .

258. Let us imagine the following case. I want to keep a diary about the recurrence of a certain sensation. To this end I associate it with the sign 'S' and write this sign in a calendar for every day on which I have the sensation. —I will remark first of all that a definition of the sign cannot be formulated. —But still I can give myself a kind of ostensive definition. —How? Can I point to the sensation? Not in the ordinary sense. But I speak, or write the sign down, and at the same time I concentrate my attention on the sensation – and so, as it were, point to it inwardly. —But what is this ceremony for? For that is all it seems to be! A definition surely serves to establish the meaning of a sign. —Well, that is done precisely by the concentration of my attention; for in this way I impress on myself the connection between the sign and the sensation. —But 'I impress it on myself' can only mean: this process brings it about that I remember the connection *right* in the future. But in the present case I have no criterion of correctness. One would like to say: whatever is going to seem right to me is right. And that only means that here we can't talk about 'right'.

. . .

265. Let us imagine a table (something like a dictionary) that exists only in our imagination. A dictionary can be used to justify the translation of word X by a word Y. But are we also to call it a justification if such a table is to be looked up only

in the imagination? —'Well, yes; then it is a subjective justification.' —But justification consists in appealing to
something independent. —'But surely I can appeal from one
memory to another. For example, I don't know if I have
remembered the time of departure of a train right and to
check it I call to mind how a page of the timetable looked.
Isn't it the same here?' —No, for this process has got to produce a memory which is actually *correct*. If the mental image
of the timetable could not itself be *tested* for correctness,
how could it confirm the correctness of the first memory? (As
if someone were to buy several copies of the morning paper
to assure himself that what it said was true.)

Looking up a table in the imagination is no more looking
up a table than the image of the result of an imagined
experiment is the result of an experiment.

. . .

293. If I say of myself that it is only from my own case that
I know what the word 'pain' means – must I not say the
same of other people too? And how can I generalize the *one*
case so irresponsibly?

Now someone tells me that *he* knows what pain is only
from his own case! —Suppose everyone had a box with
something in it: we call it a 'beetle'. No one can look into
anyone else's box, and everyone says he knows what a
beetle is only by looking at *his* beetle. —Here it would be
quite possible for everyone to have something different in
his box. One might even imagine such a thing constantly
changing. —But suppose the word 'beetle' had a use in
these people's language? —If so it would not be used as
the name of a thing. The thing in the box has no place in
the language game at all; not even as a *something*: for the
box might even be empty. —No, one can 'divide through'

by the thing in the box; it cancels out, whatever it is.

That is to say: if we construe the grammar of the expression of sensation on the model of 'object and designation' the object drops out of consideration as irrelevant.

. . .

307. 'Are you not really a behaviourist in disguise? Aren't you at bottom really saying that everything except human behaviour is a fiction?' —If I do speak of a fiction, then it is of a *grammatical* fiction.

Philosophical Investigations, 1953

The 'Private Language Argument' has become the best known and the most celebrated section of *Philosophical Investigations*. So impressed are some philosophers by this argument that they regard its conclusion – that there can be no such thing as a private language – as the nearest thing philosophy has ever had to a 'result' (in the sense in which a proven theorem in logic or mathematics is a 'result').

However, there is some controversy about what the 'Private Language Argument' is, which sections of the book contain it, and what, exactly, it is designed to establish. Almost everybody agrees that the argument begins at paragraph 243, but where it ends, nobody seems quite sure. Paragraph 315 is often given as its final paragraph, but, as I am sure most people would agree, there is some arbitrariness in this choice.

The American philosopher Saul Kripke regards the section 243–315, not as the 'Private Language Argument' itself, but as an elaboration of it. The argument itself, Kripke thinks, is contained in paragraph 202: 'And hence also "obeying a rule" is a practice. And to *think* one is obeying a rule is not to obey a rule. Hence it is not possible to obey a rule "privately": otherwise thinking one was obeying a rule would be the same thing as obeying it.' What is appealing about this paragraph, not only to Kripke but to many other philosophers as well, is that it is, at least, identifiable as an *argument*, whereas most of the section that is more conventionally regarded as the 'Private Language Argument' does not seem to centre on an argument at all; rather, it seems to be a mixed bag of bald assertions, metaphors, wry jokes and exercises of the imagination.

If we are happy to call a section of the book an 'argument' when it is manifestly *not* what is normally called an argument – that is, the premises and even the conclusion of this alleged argument seem strangely elusive – then what are we to regard as the *target* of the section beginning at paragraph 243? Some people hold that its target is the entire tradition of Western philosophy from the early modern period inaugurated by Descartes to the middle of the twentieth century. Indeed, Wittgenstein's greatest achievement, it is often said, was to have undone 300 years of Cartesianism.

Others, pointing out that Wittgenstein never read Descartes and had a frankly dismissive attitude towards the history of his subject, hold that his target was none other than Bertrand Russell. For, whoever thought that there *could* be a private language? The question is hardly one that looms large in philosophical debate at *any* time in the history of Western philosophy. And yet, in his 1918 *Lectures on Logical Atomism*, we find Russell arguing that a 'logically perfect language' would be one that was 'very largely private to one speaker'. Russell's argument for this strange conclusion goes like this:

> A moment ago I was speaking about the great advantages that we derive from the logical imperfections of language, from the fact that our words are all ambiguous. I propose now to consider what sort of language a logically perfect

language would be. In a logically perfect language the words in a proposition would correspond one by one with the components of the corresponding fact, with the exception of such words as 'or', 'not', 'if', 'then', which have a different function. In a logically perfect language, there will be one word and no more for every simple object, and everything that is not simple will be expressed by a combination of words, by a combination derived, of course, from the words for the simple things that enter in, one word for each simple component. A language of that sort will be completely analytic, and will show at a glance the logical structure of the facts asserted or denied. The language which is set forth in *Principia Mathematica* is intended to be a language of that sort. It is a language which has only syntax and no vocabulary whatsoever. Barring the omission of a vocabulary I maintain that it is quite a nice language. It aims at being the sort of language that, if you add a vocabulary, would be a logically perfect language. Actual languages are not logically perfect in this sense, and they cannot possibly be, if they are to serve the purposes of daily life. A logically perfect language, if it could be constructed, would not only be intolerably prolix, but, as regards its vocabulary, would be very largely private to one speaker. That is to say, all the names that it would use would be private to that speaker and could not enter into the language of another speaker. It could not use proper names for Socrates or Piccadilly or Rumania for the reasons I went into earlier in the lecture [that all of these things are complex, not simple, and therefore in need of analysis into their constituent parts]. Altogether you would find that it would be a very inconvenient language indeed.

Russell, *Logic and Knowledge*

Is *this* what Wittgenstein had in mind when he considered the possibility or otherwise of a private language? I think Russell's passage is useful to anyone wanting to understand the 'Private Language Argument' in that it shows a major philosopher actually entertaining the notion that a language (albeit one that was intolerably prolix, no use for daily life and altogether very inconvenient) might be private to a single speaker. However, Russell's grounds for saying that this 'logically perfect language' would be private are so idiosyncratic that they are perhaps peculiar to him. To accept these grounds would be to accept both Russell's logical atomism *and* his particular brand of solipsistic empiricism. The atomism is required to motivate the hunt for things that are 'simple' in the sense that they are not and cannot be constructed out of anything smaller, and the solipsistic empiricism is required to defend the view that those 'simples' could only be private sense-data. One further needs to adopt a referential theory of meaning, because only then would one insist that the meanings of the words in one's language had to be the *things* to which the words of language refer.

Some of Wittgenstein's remarks on the possibility of a private language would indeed be applicable to Russell's 'logically perfect language'. The argument at 202 discussed by Kripke, for example, would be enough to scupper the idea that the rules of this language could be followed privately. The somewhat similar considerations outlined in paragraph 258 concerning the imagined diary and those discussed in paragraph 265 in connection with the imaginary table for testing one's memory would also be apposite. Together, they would seem to show that what Russell purports to be merely 'intolerably prolix' and 'very inconvenient' is, in fact, incoherent. There can be no such thing as the private language imagined by Russell, because the only criteria for the correct or incorrect uses of the words of this language would be private criteria. And, as Wittgenstein argues in 202 and demonstrates with brilliant analogies in the other two paragraphs mentioned, private criteria are no criteria at all.

It is hard to believe, however, that the target of Wittgenstein's remarks in the section 243–315 is the fairly small one of Russell's deeply idiosyncratic views about the nature of a logically perfect language. It would be uncharacteristic of Wittgenstein, indeed it would run counter to his entire conception of what he was up to in his later work, for him to engage at such length in an argument *against* the views of another philosopher.

My own view is that it is best to forget that these sections of *Philosophical Investigations* – which contain some of the most innovative metaphors and some of the most inspired writing of the entire book – are supposed to constitute a single sustained argument. They quite clearly do not. Rather they are attempts to approach from a variety of different angles various assumptions about private, 'inner' experience that are customarily made by professional philosophers and ordinary people alike.

For example, it is not at all unusual, even outside philosophy seminar rooms, to hear people say things like 'only I can know whether I am really in pain; another person can only surmise it' (see paragraph 246, quoted above). To say this is to forget the 'triviality' of which Wittgenstein reminds us: 'If we are using the word "to know" as it is normally used (and how else are we to use it?) then other people very often know when I am in pain.' If we then start talking about the *certainty* with which we know our own pain, then we need to be shown that what prompts such talk is a confusion between a grammatical remark and a material one. 'One plays patience by oneself' is a *grammatical* remark. 'I went to the cinema and saw the film by myself' is a *material* remark. The first might be used to explain to somebody what kind of game patience is. Similarly the sentence 'Sensations are private' is a grammatical remark; it says what kind of things sensations are, it does not, e.g., report a possible *discovery* about sensations.

There is a tendency – and, again, like the 'picture of the essence of human language' discernible in Augustine's description of how he learned to speak, this is a *pre*-philosophical tendency rather than a philosophical *opinion* – to think that the private is somehow logically prior to the public. 'I know what *I* see, think, feel, etc.,' it is common to believe, 'but I have to *infer* what you or anybody else is seeing, thinking, feeling, etc.' One of Wittgenstein's aims in *Philosophical Investigations* is to show the incoherence of this picture of the relative priority of the private and the public. This is the point of the famous 'beetle in the box' of paragraph 293 (quoted above). The thing (the beetle, or whatever) to which *only* I have access *cannot* be the meaning – or even the reference – of words that have a public use. And, as words like 'belief', 'desire', 'intention', 'thought', etc. undeniably have a public use, it follows that neither their reference nor their meaning can possibly be something essentially private.

As Wittgenstein anticipated (see 307 above), he was interpreted as a behaviourist, as someone who believed that we had to accept that what we meant by pain was simply the behaviour characteristic of someone in pain *and nothing else*. In paragraph 304 he tried to pull the rug from under this egregious misunderstanding:

> 'But you will surely admit that there is a difference between pain-behaviour accompanied by pain and pain-

behaviour without any pain?' —Admit it? What greater difference could there be? —'And yet you again and again
reach the conclusion that the sensation itself is a *nothing*.'
—Not at all. It is not a *something*, but not a *nothing* either!
The conclusion was only that a nothing would serve just as
well as a something about which nothing could be said. We
have only rejected the grammar which tries to force itself
on us here.

The paradox disappears only if we make a radical break
with the idea that language always functions in one way,
always serves the same purpose: to convey thoughts –
which may be about houses, pains, good and evil, or anything else you please.

The mistake Wittgenstein himself made in *Tractatus Logico-Philosophicus* and the mistake Augustine made in *Confessions* is the mistake we *all* make when we want to counter behaviourism with some suggestion of the sort that thoughts, desires, etc. are not *nothing*. No, they are not nothing, and they are not identical with behaviour either. But neither are they *things*, and the only reason we want them to be things is that we are committed to a faulty view of language, one that thinks that to every meaningful word there must correspond some *object*. *Philosophical Investigations* – indeed, Wittgenstein's entire later philosophy – begins and ends with an attack on this misunderstanding about the nature of language. But it is not the kind of mistake that can be dispensed with once and for all with a single argument, because it reappears in different contexts under different guises, which is why it cannot effectively be opposed with a *doctrine*.

10

READING WITTGENSTEIN IN THE RIGHT SPIRIT

This book is written for those who are in sympathy with the spirit in which it is written. This is not, I believe, the spirit of the main current of European and American civilization. The spirit of this civilization makes itself manifest in the industry, architecture and music of our time, in its fascism and socialism, and it is alien and uncongenial to the author. This is not a value judgment. It is not, it is true, as though he accepted what nowadays passes for architecture as architecture or did not approach what is called modern music with the greatest suspicion (though without understanding its language), but still, the disappearance of the arts does not justify judging disparagingly the human beings who make up this civilization. For in times like these, genuine strong characters simply leave the arts aside and turn to other things and somehow the worth of the individual man finds expression. Not, to be sure, in the way it would at a time of high culture. A culture is like a big organization which assigns each of its members a place where he can work in the spirit of the whole; and it is perfectly fair for his power to be measured by the contribution he succeeds in making to the whole enterprise. In an age without culture on the other hand forces become fragmented and the power of an individual man is used up in overcoming opposing forces and frictional resistances; it does not show in the distance he travels but perhaps only in the heat he generates in overcoming friction. But energy is still energy and even if the spectacle which our age affords us is not the formation of a great cultural work, with the best men contributing to the same great end, so much as the unimpressive spectacle of a crowd whose best members work for purely private ends, still we must not forget that the spectacle is not what matters.

I realize then that the disappearance of a culture does not signify the disappearance of human value, but simply of certain means of expressing this value, yet the fact remains that I have no sympathy for the current of European civilization and do not understand its goals, if it has any. So I am really writing for friends who are scattered throughout the corners of the globe.

It is all one to me whether or not the typical western scientist understands or appreciates my work, since he will not in any case understand the spirit in which I write. Our civilization is characterized by the word 'progress'. Progress is its form rather than making progress being one of its features. Typically it constructs. It is occupied with building an ever more complicated structure. And even clarity is sought only as a means to this end, not as an end in itself. For me on the contrary clarity, perspicuity are valuable in themselves.

I am not interested in constructing a building, so much as in having a perspicuous view of the foundations of possible buildings.

So, I am not aiming at the same target as the scientists
and my way of thinking is different from theirs.

Early draft of the Foreword to *Philosophical Remarks*, 1930

Reading the later Wittgenstein as a behaviourist is analogous to reading the early Wittgenstein as a Logical Positivist. In both cases, it is a mistake that could not possibly be made by anybody who knew Wittgenstein or who understood what kind of man he was. And, just as Paul Engelmann decided to publish his correspondence with Wittgenstein in order to counteract what he knew were fundamental misconceptions about the *Tractatus*, so Wittgenstein's Cambridge friend, Maurice Drury, decided to publish notes of his conversations with Wittgenstein of the 1930s and 1940s in order to correct the effect of, as he put it, 'well-meaning commentators' who 'make it appear that his writings were now easily assimilable into the very intellectual milieu they were largely a warning against'.

Drury's conversations with Wittgenstein are invaluable for showing what *really* interested him. They abound with reflections on ethics, religion and culture and show how deeply opposed Wittgenstein was to the worship of science characteristic of our age. They also show – what is almost entirely absent from Wittgenstein's philosophical writings – how much Wittgenstein venerated the great composers of the classical age. A typical episode recounted by Drury concerns an occasion when Wittgenstein came to see him looking very distressed. When Drury asked what was the matter, Wittgenstein replied:

I was walking about in Cambridge and passed a bookshop and in the window were portraits of Russell, Freud and Einstein. A little further on, in a music shop, I saw portraits

of Beethoven, Schubert and Chopin. Comparing these portraits I felt intensely the terrible degeneration that had come
over the human spirit in the course of only a hundred years.

Wittgenstein worried deeply that what he cared most about
had found no direct expression in his philosophical writing, so
leaving him open to being fundamentally misunderstood. 'It
is impossible for me to say one word in my book about all that
music has meant in my life,' he once told Drury. 'How then
can I hope to be understood?'

This is why he wrote the kind of preface quoted above: to
try to communicate the *spirit* in which he wrote and to say
how important it was to him that that spirit not only was
not the same as the spirit which informs modern Western
civilization, but was actually *opposed* to it.

On the other hand, he was aware of a certain kind of
paradox involved in this:

> Telling someone something he does not understand is
> pointless, even if you add that he will not understand it.
> (That so often happens with someone you love.) If you
> have a room which you do not want certain people to get
> into, put a lock on it for which they do not have the key.
> But there is no point in talking to them about it, unless
> of course you want them to admire the room from the
> outside!
>
> The honourable thing to do is to put a lock on the door
> which will be noticed only by those who can open it, not by
> the rest.

'But,' he added, 'it's proper to say that I think the book has
nothing to do with the progressive civilization of Europe and

America. And that while its spirit may be possible only in the surroundings of this civilization, they have different objectives.'

That Wittgenstein was right to be concerned that the spirit in which he wrote was understood is attested by the fact that, even now, after the publication of Engelmann's memoir, of Drury's conversations and of Wittgenstein's various drafts of a preface to *Philosophical Remarks*, philosophical views are still being attributed to him that (a) he could not possibly have held, given his general *Weltanschauung* and (b) are, as Drury put it, part of the milieu against which his work is a warning.

11

UNDERSTANDING OTHERS, UNDERSTANDING OURSELVES: IMPONDERABLE EVIDENCE

Is there such a thing as 'expert judgment' about the genuineness of expressions of feeling? —Even here there are those whose judgment is 'better' and those whose judgment is 'worse'.

Correcter prognoses will generally issue from the judgments of those with better knowledge of mankind.

Can one learn this knowledge? Yes; some can. Not, however, by taking a course in it, but through '*experience*'. —Can someone else be a man's teacher in this? Certainly. From time to time he gives him the right *tip*. —This is what 'learning' and 'teaching' are like here. —What one acquires here is not a technique; one learns correct judgments. There are also rules, but they do not form a system, and only experienced people can apply them right. Unlike calculating-rules.

What is most difficult here is to put this indefiniteness, correctly and unfalsified, into words . . .

It is certainly possible to be convinced by evidence that someone is in such-and-such a state of mind, that, for instance, he is not pretending. But 'evidence' here includes 'imponderable' evidence.

The question is: what does imponderable evidence *accomplish*?

Suppose there were imponderable evidence for the chemical (internal) structure of a substance, still it would have to prove itself to be evidence by certain consequences which *can* be weighed.

(Imponderable evidence might convince someone that a picture was a genuine . . . But it is *possible* for this to be proved right by documentary evidence as well.)

Imponderable evidence includes subtleties of glance, of gesture, of tone.

I may recognize a genuine loving look, distinguish it from a pretended one (and here there can, of course, be a 'ponderable' confirmation of my judgment). But I may be quite incapable of describing the difference. And this is not because the languages I know have no words for it. For why not introduce new words? —If I were a very talented painter I might conceivably represent the genuine and the simulated glance in pictures.

Ask yourself: How does a man learn to get a 'nose' for something? And how can this nose be used?

Philosophical Investigations, Part II

What is now Part II of *Philosophical Investigations* is a collection of remarks on the philosophy of psychology that represents a very small selection from the manuscripts on the subject that Wittgenstein wrote in the last few years of his life. These manuscripts have now been published as *Remarks on the Philosophy of Psychology* and *Last Writings on the Philosophy of Psychology*. They are extraordinarily interesting, not least for the light they throw on the suggestive remarks about 'imponderable evidence' that appear at the end of *Philosophical Investigations*.

I have emphasized that one of Wittgenstein's central themes in his later work is the importance of preserving the integrity of a *non-scientific* form of understanding, the kind of understanding characteristic of the arts and the kind of understanding that Goethe, Spengler and Wittgenstein sought to protect from the encroachment of science and scientism. One of the most important differences between the method of science and the non-theoretical understanding that is exemplified in music, art, philosophy and ordinary life, is that science aims at a level of generality that necessarily eludes these other forms of understanding. And this is why the understanding of people can never be a science. To understand a person is to be able to tell, for example, whether he means what he says or not, whether his expressions of feeling are genuine or feigned. And how does one acquire *this* sort of understanding? This is the question Wittgenstein raises in the remarks quoted above.

The evidence upon which *expert* judgments about people are based is, according to Wittgenstein, 'imponderable', resistant to the general formulation characteristic of science, or even to the weighing up characteristic of legal evidence.

But the fact that we are dealing here with imponderables should not mislead us into believing that all claims to understand people are spurious or built upon shaky foundations. When Wittgenstein was once discussing his favourite novel, *The Brothers Karamazov*, with his friend Maurice Drury, Drury mentioned that he found the character of Father Zossima extremely impressive. Of Zossima, Dostoevsky writes:

> It was said that, by permitting everyone for so many years to come to bare their hearts and beg his advice and healing words, he had absorbed so many secrets, sorrows, and

avowals into his soul that in the end he had acquired so
fine a perception that he could tell at the first glance from
the face of a stranger what he had come for, what he
wanted and what kind of torment racked his conscience.

When Drury read this passage out, Wittgenstein remarked:
'Yes, there really have been people like that, who could see
directly into the souls of other people and advise them.'

'An inner process stands in need of outward criteria' runs
one of the most often quoted aphorisms of *Philosophical
Investigations*, an aphorism that many have cited in support of
the notion that Wittgenstein was some sort of behaviourist, an
interpretation that needs to be resisted. One way of resisting it
is to realize what an emphasis Wittgenstein placed on the
need for sensitive perception of those 'outward criteria' in all
their imponderability. And where does one find such acute
sensitivity? Not, typically, in the works of psychologists, but in
those of the great artists, musicians and novelists. 'People
nowadays,' Wittgenstein writes in *Culture and Value*, 'think
that scientists exist to instruct them, poets, musicians, etc. to
give them pleasure. The idea *that these have something to teach
them* – that does not occur to them.' What *do* they have to
teach us? Well, to name one crucially important thing: the
importance of imponderable evidence for an understanding of
the people around us.

The notion of 'imponderable evidence' is somewhat slippery, and there are signs that Wittgenstein himself was, at
times at least, somewhat sceptical of it. In one of the manuscripts published as *Last Writings on the Philosophy of Psychology*,
he asks himself: 'What does "*imponderable* evidence" mean?'
adding, as if determined to come clean: 'Let's be honest!' He
goes on:

I tell someone that I have reasons for this claim or proofs for it, but that they are 'imponderable'.

Well, *for instance*, I have seen the look which one person has given another. I say 'If you had seen it you would have said the same thing.' Some other time perhaps, I might get him to see this look, and then he will be convinced. That would be *one* possibility.

What does imponderable evidence *accomplish*? And: What entitles one to call it 'evidence'? The answers he gives are perhaps disappointingly opaque:

An important fact here is that we learn certain things only through long experience and not from a course in school. How, for instance, does one develop the eye of a connoisseur? Someone says, for example, 'This picture was not painted by such-and-such a master' – the statement he makes is thus not an aesthetic judgment, but one that can be proved by documentation. He may not be able to give any good reasons for his verdict. —How did he learn it? Could someone have taught him? Yes. —Not in the same way as one learns to calculate. A great deal of experience was necessary. That is, the learner probably had to look at and compare a large number of pictures by various masters again and again. In doing this he could have been given hints. Well, that was the process of learning. But then he looked at a picture and made a judgment about it. In most cases he was able to list his reasons for his judgment, but generally it wasn't they that were convincing.

Two paragraphs later: 'A *connoisseur* couldn't make himself understood to a jury, for instance. That is, they would understand his statement, but not his reasons. He can give intimations to another connoisseur, and the latter will understand them.'

So what *does* 'imponderable evidence' mean? Well, it is evidence that has these characteristics:

1. it can be *seen* as evidence for a particular judgment, but usually it cannot be described other than as evidence for that judgment (e.g., 'How do you *know* your father dislikes your boyfriend?' 'I could tell by the way he looked at him' 'And how did he look at him?' 'Well, . . . as if he didn't like him')

2. the value of the evidence varies with the experience and the knowledge of the person providing it, and this is more or less the *only* way of weighing such evidence, since

3. it cannot be evaluated, weighed, *pondered*, by appeal to any system of general principles or universal laws.

In all these respects it stands in stark contrast to *scientific* evidence.

The notion of imponderable evidence serves in Wittgenstein's final writings as a way of distancing him from, on the one hand, those who look to science to provide psychological insight, and, on the other, those in the humanities who have become convinced that understanding another person, having access to their inner life, is impossible. In philosophical discussions of biography, it is sometimes claimed that (to quote the biographer and literary theorist David Ellis): 'Discovering what someone is like involves, among many other things, attempting to reconstruct what has been called their internal soliloquy.' As we have no access to anybody's 'internal soliloquy' but our own, Ellis calls the claim that we can understand another human being an 'affable pretence'.

Wittgenstein's last writings on the philosophy of psychology are extremely useful in warding off this untenable scepticism. Take this from *Last Writings on the Philosophy of Psychology: The Inner and the Outer, Volume 2*:

> Why can't you be certain that someone is not pretending? —'Because one cannot look into him.' —But if you could, what would you see there? —'His secret thoughts.' —But if he only utters them in Chinese – where do you have to look then? —'But I cannot be certain that he is uttering them truthfully!' —But where do you have to look to find out whether he is uttering them truthfully?
>
> Even if I were now to hear everything that he is saying to himself, I would know as little what his words were referring to as if I read *one* sentence in the middle of a story. Even if I knew everything now going on within him, I still wouldn't know, for example, to whom the names and images in his thoughts related.

'It's only in particular cases that the inner is hidden from me,' Wittgenstein reminds us a few pages later, 'and in those cases it is not hidden because it is inner.'

'Indeed, often,' he says, 'I can describe [a person's] inner, as I perceive it, but not his outer.' He does not give any examples, but it is not difficult to think of the kind of thing he has in mind. If somebody asks me how my son looked when he finished the computer game he had been playing all summer, I might reply: 'He looked pleased and triumphant.' If somebody asked me how my daughter looked on her first day at school, I would reply: 'She looked nervous and hesitant.'

To say of somebody that they are nervous, hesitant, pleased or triumphant is to attribute to them a mental state, and, therefore, according to people like David Ellis, to engage in the 'affable pretence' of having access to another person's 'inner' feelings. But, when we talk like that, we are forgetting that these words are used in a perfectly ordinary way to describe how people *look*, and, therefore, in some sense their 'outer appearance'.

What is so wonderful about Wittgenstein's last writings on psychology is that they preserve in all their nuances the rich variety of psychological descriptions of other people that we have at our disposal. The 'grammatical fictions' he had exposed in the first half of the *Investigations* are shown to be of the utmost importance because they get in the way, not just of philosophical clarity, but of a full understanding of art, music, literature and, above all, ourselves.

CHRONOLOGY

26 April 1889, born in Vienna, the eighth and youngest child of Karl and Leopoldine Wittgenstein.

1903–06, attends the Realschule at Linz.

1906–08, studies mechanical engineering at the Technische Hochschule in Charlottenburg, Berlin.

1908–11, studies aeronautical engineering at Manchester.

1911, arrives in Cambridge to study with Bertrand Russell.

1913, publishes a review of Coffey, *The Science of Logic* in the *Cambridge Magazine.*

1913–14, lives alone in Norway, where he works on solving the problems of logic.

June 1914, arrives in Vienna, with the intention of returning to Norway after the summer.

1914–18, fights for the Austrian army on, first, the Russian Front and, then, the Italian Front.

1918–19, spends a year as Italian prisoner of war; finishes *Tractatus Logico-Philosophicus.*

1919–20, trains as a schoolteacher in Vienna.

1920–22, teaches at an elementary school in Trattenbach, Lower Austria; *Tractatus Logico-Philosophicus* is published.

1922–24, teaches at an elementary school in Puchberg; is visited by Frank Ramsey.

1924–26, teaches at an elementary school in Otterthal.

1926–28, works as an architect in Vienna.

1929, returns to Cambridge to study with Frank Ramsey.

1930, Ramsey dies.

1930, Wittgenstein starts lecturing at Cambridge.

1933–34, dictates *The Blue Book* to his students instead of lecturing.

1934–35, dictates *The Brown Book* to a select group of students.

1935, visits the Soviet Union.

1936–37, lives in Norway, where he writes much of what is now Part I of *Philosophical Investigations.*

12 March 1938, *Anschluss* between Austria and Nazi Germany; Wittgenstein becomes a German citizen.

April 1938, becomes a British citizen.

11 February 1939, elected Professor of Philosophy at the University of Cambridge.

1941–42, works as a porter at Guy's Hospital, London.

1942–44, works as a laboratory assistant on a medical research project at Newcastle.

1944–47, lectures at Cambridge.

1947, resigns his Cambridge professorship.

1947–49, lives in Ireland, where he writes what is now Part II of *Philosophical Investigations.*

1950, visits Austria for the last time.

28 April 1951, dies in Cambridge.

SUGGESTIONS FOR FURTHER READING

Primary Material

'Review of P. Coffey, *The Science of Logic*', *Cambridge Review*, XXXIV (1913), p. 351

Notebooks on Logic 1914–16, eds. G.E.M. Anscombe and G.H. von Wright, Oxford, Blackwell, 1961

Tractatus Logico-Philosophicus, trans. C.K. Ogden and F.P. Ramsey, London, Routledge, 1922

Tractatus Logico-Philosophicus, trans. D.F. Pears and B.F. McGuinness, London, Routledge, 1961

'Some Remarks on Logical Form', *Proceedings of the Aristotelian Society*, IX, 1929, pp. 162–71

'A Lecture on Ethics', *Philosophical Review*, LXXIV, 1968, pp. 4–14

Philosophical Remarks, Oxford, Blackwell, 1975

Philosophical Grammar, Oxford, Blackwell, 1974

The Blue and Brown Books, Oxford, Blackwell, 1975

Remarks on the Foundations of Mathematics, Oxford, Blackwell, 1967

Philosophical Investigations, Oxford, Blackwell, 1953

Remarks on the Philosophy of Psychology, I, Oxford, Blackwell, 1980

Remarks on the Philosophy of Psychology, II, Oxford, Blackwell, 1980

Last Writings on the Philosophy of Psychology, I, Oxford, Blackwell, 1982

Last Writings on the Philosophy of Psychology, II, Oxford, Blackwell, 2001

Secondary Material

Carey, Alice and Rupert Read, eds., *The New Wittgenstein*, London, Routledge, 2000

Conant, James, 'The Method of the *Tractatus*', in Erich H. Reck, ed., *From Frege to Wittgenstein: Perspectives on Early Analytic Philosophy*, New York, OUP, 2002, pp. 374–462

Diamond, Cora, *The Realistic Spirit*, Cambridge, Mass., MIT Press, 1991

Drury, M. O'C., *The Danger of Words*, London, Routledge, 1973

Ellis, David, *Literary Lives*, Edinburgh University Press, 2000

Engelmann, Paul, *Letters from Ludwig Wittgenstein with a Memoir*, Oxford, Blackwell, 1967

Kripke, Saul, *Wittgenstein on Rules and Private Language*, Oxford, Blackwell, 1984

Monk, Ray, *Ludwig Wittgenstein: The Duty of Genius*, London, Cape, 1990

Ramsey, F.P., 'Critical Notice of L. Wittgenstein's *Tractatus Logico-Philosophicus*', *Mind*, XXXII, October 1923, pp. 465–78

Russell, Bertrand, *Logic and Knowledge: Essays 1901–1950*, London, Routledge, 1992

INDEX